Fate or Destiny?

Also by Nano Daemon

Meet Jesus the Alchemist – The Next Evolutionary Step for Humanity

The Seventh Sense – Your GPS to the Cosmos

Question and Answer Series:

Book 1: *What's Death Got to do with Living? - Discover the Other Side of Reality, Consciousness, and the Afterlife.*

Book 2: *Discovering Your Psychic Senses – Harness your Imagination, Meditation, and Self-Hypnosis to Attain Psychic Perception.*

Book 3: *The Alchemy of Transformation – How are Evolution, the Law of Attraction, The Matrix, or Witchcraft related?*

Fate or Destiny?

Journeys into the SuperNatural
and
Realities Beyond

A True Story

− Nano Daemon −

Calico Graphics and Images Caleb Jorge (Illustrator)
Sherrie Dolby (Editor)

BALBOA.
PRESS

A DIVISION OF HAY HOUSE

Calico Graphics and Images Caleb Jorge (Illustrator)
Edited by Sherrie Dolby dolbyduranduran@yahoo.com

Balboa Press books may be ordered through booksellers or by contacting:

Balboa Press
A Division of Hay House
1663 Liberty Drive
Bloomington, IN 47403
www.balboapress.com
1 (877) 407-4847

Because of the dynamic nature of the Internet, any web addresses or links contained in this book may have changed since publication and may no longer be valid. The views expressed in this work are solely those of the author and do not necessarily reflect the views of the publisher, and the publisher hereby disclaims any responsibility for them.

The author of this book does not dispense medical advice or prescribe the use of any technique as a form of treatment for physical, emotional, or medical problems without the advice of a physician, either directly or indirectly. The intent of the author is only to offer information of a general nature to help you in your quest for emotional and spiritual well-being. In the event you use any of the information in this book for yourself, which is your constitutional right, the author and the publisher assume no responsibility for your actions.

Any people depicted in stock imagery provided by Thinkstock are models, and such images are being used for illustrative purposes only.
Certain stock imagery © Thinkstock.

Printed in the United States of America.

ISBN: 978-1-4525-1809-1 (sc)
ISBN: 978-1-4525-1811-4 (hc)
ISBN: 978-1-4525-1810-7 (e)

Library of Congress Control Number: 2014912249

Balboa Press rev. date: 07/11/2014

Dedication

To my Invisible Friends Beyond.

As Above, So Below

Below is the Natural World. Above is the SuperNatural World

Table of Contents

Preface

Journeys into the SuperNatural and Realities Beyond is the step-by-step depiction of my encounters with the Supernatural world. It starts with the day my life turned upside down and its gradual progression into psychic phenomena, and finally the exhilarating, and often hilarious, experiences of being ushered into the spiritual spectrum of reality.

Why is it that when you think you've got it all, your life turns upside down?
Why is it that life in retrospect looks so totally different?
Why is it that life makes sense only in retrospect?

Is life pre-determined?
Is our destiny inevitable?

These were all questions that plagued me and sent me spinning in Search of Clues as my world as I knew it had turned on its axis. My heavenly abode consisting of a terrestrial paradise was destroyed and hell loomed on the horizon.

My entire belief system was shattered and I wished I would "wake up dead."

In the interior of my world, scraps of memories floated to the surface, leaving imprints that led me on a path where the SuperNatural was awaiting me with its magical tricks. I was gradually awakened to new dimensions of reality that led me on an enchanting and fun-filled journey of self-discovery and discovery of ancient knowledge.

I discovered that the SuperNatural was simply the Superior form of the Natural.

PART I

Life in Retro

RECALL 1

I remember precisely the day my life turned upside down.

I had reached the summit of my dreams, without much effort it seemed. I had it all and was at the prime of my life: a loving husband who, for 10 years, never missed a day without telling me "I love you," the most beautiful and brilliant child who never gave me any trouble despite the fact that I did not have one ounce of motherly instinct before his appearance in my life, an architect-designed 6-level home nestled in the tree tops of the bush, with serene water views, in a prestigious suburb, in one of the most coveted cities of the world, a Porsche, designer label clothes, an enviable social life and a thriving business in the self-development field with my husband.

I was healthy, happy, and blissfully unaware.

This particular day, I was in the garden working out the finishing touches to the swimming pool that we had just put in. It was designed to match the contours of the peaceful water view which greeted my eyes through the French doors of our bedroom first thing in the morning as I opened my eyes. The doorbell rang and I leaped 6 levels to the top front door wondering who it could be, as most of the 8 doors leading outdoors were usually left open throughout the day and our friends would amble in through the lower ones without knocking.

I opened the door to three of Jehovah's Witnesses brandishing a book in my face and asking if I wanted to be shown the way to eternal life. "Eternal life!" I screamed with all the breath left in my lungs after my steep climb.

"Who wants eternal life? Death is salvation!!!" and I slammed the door, not before I gleaned the horrified expressions on all 3 faces.

The horror on their faces was nothing compared to the horror I felt at my own outburst, at my behaviour, and at the words I had uttered.

Death is salvation? Salvation from what? Where were these words coming from? What possessed me to behave in such a manner which was so contrary to my usual self? Running up 6 flights, though annoying, hardly qualified for such an outburst.

The words "death is salvation," with their ominous ring in my ears, kept playing in my head in a loop excluding all possibility of any other thought. Gone were the brilliant ideas I was revelling in for the creation of paradise around our swimming pool. A feeling of doom surrounded me, and I was drained of all energy. I dragged myself to my bed and just managed to throw myself on it. I noticed a crystal a friend had given me the day before on my bedside table. My hand reached out and grasped it. I felt I was leaving this world. My eyes closed, and I witnessed the most beautiful vision.

In my vision, I saw an ellipse against a beautiful clear blue sky. Along this ellipse were interspersed a boat, a house, trees, and flowers as well as other representations of what I cherished in life. There was also one big fluffy white cloud, which I called Cloud 9, and which is where I usually hang out in my daydreaming states. I was sitting on this cloud with a great big smile on my face basking in bliss, when suddenly I heard a loud roar. I dug my fingers into the cloud hanging on for my life. The cloud detached itself from the ellipse, turned upside down, and I started the fall. A long, long, very long fall, fraught with panic and terror, which seemed to take an eternity. This was no dream or daydream.

When I finally hit the bed and bounced off, I felt like every bone in my body was shattered and my entire body was writhing in pain. The physical and emotional pain lasted for hours. My mind went numb.

Within a week my marriage was over and the process of disintegration had set in. I found out my husband was having an affair, and I had had no inkling of it whatsoever.

... And little did I know then, the meaning of my own thoughts and experiences.

~~~~

RECALL 2

Though my vision had prepared me for doom, I could not come to terms with what was happening. This was the last thing I expected. There had been no preliminaries, no reason, and no clues. Could I have been so blind, so stupid?

Not only was my husband betraying me, but two of my best friends were conspiring with him to break up my marriage; friends that I loved and trusted with all my heart and spent countless hours helping them in their times of need. How could they turn against me? What had I done?

The closest I came to an answer was when I confronted my dearest friend and reminded her that when her husband was having an affair I was the one who talked to him and turned him around to see the error of his ways and saved their marriage. Why was she doing this to me?

"Oh," she said in a dismissive voice. "That's because you're perfect and I am not!"

Thinking was futile. Nothing made sense. As time went by, it seemed like the whole world was conspiring to end my marriage which, to me, was absolutely sacred, and my home, family, and relationship to them were the things I valued above all else in life.

First I went into denial trying to prove to myself I was wrong, I was misreading, misinterpreting the events. But my best friends, and the taunting anonymous phone calls which I failed to connect, were all keen to prove my marriage was over.

When I finally confronted my husband, he first denied all allegations, then threatened to actually proceed with the affair since he was being accused of it anyway, then put the entire blame for the failure of our marriage upon my weakened shoulders.

The only serious explanation I ever got was: "This is not a house we live in, it's a showroom." He also proceeded to mimic the way I combed my hair and put on lipstick to appear attractive at all times, insinuating that was all I cared about.

Did it ever occur to him I wanted to give him the very best that I had?

What about running our business behind the scenes, taking care of all the sundry details: clients, phone calls, correspondence, accounts, taxation, legal matters, and whatever drama arose, so everything would run smoothly and so he could shine on stage and take all the credit?

What about all the hands-on heavy work I did during the massive renovations we carried out on our properties while trying to maintain a lovely home he could come to, all while bringing up a child?

... Denial turned to rage.

~~~~

RECALL 3

Since my biggest sin was running a showroom, I decided to right that wrong. I stopped all the illicit contributing factors: washing, cleaning, tidying, you name it.

As the house was quite spacious, it took 6 weeks for the gap between the scattered clothes and other items discarded on the floor to get so small that it was getting more and more difficult to negotiate the next step, without tripping on something offensive.

Cooking was out of the question as there was no space left in the dishwater, the sink, or bench tops, nor was there any clean utensils.

The scene reminded me of a cartoon that had sent me into convulsive laughter: A dishevelled woman in bed, with a cigarette hanging from her mouth, reading a book, with the radio blaring on her bedside table, a scene practically identical to the one I found myself in, and her husband yelling at the top of his voice: "What's this?" To which she replies, "This is all the work I don't do every day!"

I was now reduced to this caricature of myself.

One late morning, as I lay in bed still in my nightie trying to read a novel while listening to loud music to deafen the thoughts in my head, my husband, whom I had naturally kicked out of our bedroom, burst in yelling at the top of his voice "..". The words went in one ear and out the other (thank God for two ears!) bypassing my comprehension, but I heard the concluding sentence loud and clear "I NEED A WIFE!!!"

To which my now wise self responded without any collaboration from me: "SO DO I!!!"

There seemed to be no way to please this man who was now a stranger to me.
The other stranger was I.
And stranger still was the reality of my new life.
My world had turned on its axis and the present became irrelevant.

Scraps of memories of a long distant past, which made no sense to me at the time, reinstalled themselves in the forefront of my cortex and played their tune trying to coax me into making sense of them now .... *in retrospect.*

I pushed them back, I didn't want to think. I took to alcohol, which I loathed, in the hopes of drowning them. I was too tired to fight, too tired to think.

... *But I remembered.*

~~~~

RECALL 4

I remembered Egypt, the country of my birth where I had spent the happiest days of my life as a child and a teenager. I remembered the hustle and bustle of Cairo, the city that never slept and buzzed with life for 24 hours a day. I remembered the carefree attitude of the beautiful Egyptian people who surrendered their fate to Allah and responded to how are you? with, "El hamdu lillah" translating as "gratitude to God." They cared not for material possessions and felt enormous empathy for the pain and plight of others, always ready to help a stranger on the road and expressing joy at the slightest sign of mercy Allah had thrown their way. They seemed to have discovered an endless well of happiness in the barren desert of their lives. They lived by Buddhist principles which neither they nor I had ever heard of at the time.

I could now feel the goose bumps that covered my body in the hot summer nights when we held picnics by the moonlight at the foot of the pyramids, starting at midnight, followed by horse riding at dawn.

I remembered the time the horse I had hired decided to award itself total freedom and galloped into the sunrise, leaving behind all traces of civilisation. Having no riding skills and devoid of any sense of direction, I remembered clinging to my horse for my life. I had heard that when horses get hungry they head back home and I hung all my chances of survival on that belief. As I looked around all I could see was large expanses of sand dunes with nothing else in sight but the infiniteness of a clear blue sky. I felt so small and insignificant that I decided to divert my sight away from the horizon where the 2 giants met undisturbed by any sign of civilisation.

I looked away and down and my gaze fell upon a grain of sand. The smallness of it struck my vulnerable state and I joined in empathy with the grain of sand.

Some might call this a mystical experience. To me, it was sheer terror as I felt that if I got any smaller I risked total annihilation, though the beauty and majesty of this impenetrable vastness was not wasted on me. I was 10 years old, and I survived to tell the tale.

Today, I felt again this same sense of annihilation. The annihilation of my identity. The annihilation of my value system. A thought entered my mind: Would I survive to tell this tale?

... But so little did I know then.

~~~~~

RECALL 5

Another dawn, another sleepless night, and I remembered....

I was 4½ years old, and my parents took me on a holiday to visit some friends. That's when I met Reg for the first time. I fell in love with Reg, not for who he was, but for what he represented: a boy who was allowed to do anything, ride bicycles, and climb trees.

That was it for me, all I had to do was change my name, wear pants, and chop my hair. My mother was a dressmaker, so scissors were at hand. I wore my brother's pants (girls never wore pants in Egypt then) and henceforth I would only respond to the name Reg. That was my way of claiming freedom reserved only for boys.

Freedom, independent will, and masculine attributes were goals I had established for myself by the age of 4½. That much was clear now but what did that have to do with what was happening to me?

That episode had lasted until I was 12 years old. One day, 2 women grabbed hold of me in the street and would not let go of me until I resolved their dilemma: one woman insisted I was a boy, the other I was a girl. **Little did I know in those days that androgyny was the inner state of my soul seeking expression.**

But then nature took its cruel course and fighting against my femininity became futile. So I went with the flow, did a flip-side, and fell in love with every male that walked through the door. And there were plenty of those. My older brother had an array of the most gorgeous friends that nature had created. I was in love with each and every one of them as each represented an aspect of the "me" I wished I could bring out. I was still a boy at heart and they treated me as one of them. And that was just perfect for me from the age of 12 to 17, until they all, in unison with my brother, made a dash for the lures of Brazil and its enticing promises of life, lust, and love. I was left behind.

Looking back, I am amazed at how easy I found it to transfer my enormous capacity for love to other situations, other experiences, and other adventures. Back in Egypt, love and sex were diametrically opposed, leaving love in its most innocent, all-consuming, original, and untampered state.

In conformity with my self-allocated boy privileges, at the age of 7 I had put my foot down and demanded to be taken out of the Armenian school my parents sent me to because they were both Armenian and be enrolled in a French School. It wasn't the nuns or Catholicism that attracted me; it was the sound of the French language which drew me with an irresistible force like a tune played on Pan's pipe.

From term one, Napoleon became my hero and Joan of Arc my role model. So you can imagine my bewilderment when 2 decades later my sister-in-law dragged me to a psychic who said that in one of my past life times I was Pope Joan. "Who is Pope Joan" I asked? Pope Joan was a female who passed herself off as a man to become a pope. I couldn't believe my ears.

I remembered, as a true boy, I had vowed to never cry and I held to my vow. And now, for the first time in a very long time, I was crying inconsolably, uncontrollably, and convulsively until my insides were churned out and I was vomiting blood. It did not even occur to me to consult a doctor.

... How I wished I could sleep once again.

~~~~~

RECALL 6

My wish was granted.

Next night I fell asleep but achieved no peace.

My dreams were as harrowing as my waking life. They would alternate between 2 themes. I would be driving and my wind screen would be all fogged up. I could not see where I was going, but I could not stop the car, and I was sure I was heading for a collision. In the other theme, I would be running late for an important test, the "Masters" would be waiting for me, but I was constantly held back, and I could not sit for the test. The sense of failure was daunting.

I came to realise these dreams were a vivid reflection of my life. I started taking notice of my dreams. This was probably the beginning of my journey into the dream states.

One evening, when I was helping myself to a shot of brandy, my son asked me with concern on his face, "Mummy, are you an alcoholic?" I felt like I was being stabbed in the heart. How could I have been so callous? How could I have been so self-centred and thoughtless? How could I not have seen the anxiety and sorrow I was causing him?

"No baby," I lied. "That's just medicine; I have been sick," feeling truly sick in my stomach. I put the bottle down and vowed not to touch it again.

Totally distraught by shame at the state I had allowed myself to sink into, that night I went to bed wishing "I would wake up dead."

I had a dream.

In my dream I was dead. My body was tied down with ropes and floating beneath the surface of the ocean. Floating above the ocean, I looked down and watched without emotion some fishermen pull me out of the water. I was surprised at how beautiful and serene I looked, unmarred by my immersion in the water for so long.

I noted with interest that I was tied with 3 sets of rope. One around the chest area, one around the solar plexus, and one lower down. The 2 higher ropes were cut loose, but the 3rd one was still holding my hands tied down.

... A major shift in the scenario of my life was taking place.

~~~~~

RECALL 7

True to my wish, the next day "I woke up dead." I did not die. I just woke up dead to my old world, dead to my old values, dead to my old beliefs, with a vacant mind, and no plans or desires for the future.

I did not realise at the time how strange the choice of the wording of my wish had been and how literally the Universe had responded. So little did I know in those days.

I had made a vow to bring normality to my life for my son's sake, so I went through my days mechanically making sure everything was attended to and all his needs were met. When he was at school, I spent most of my days in the bush with the Kookaburras as my companions. When I was late coming out, they would knock on my window or come into the house to fetch me. I lost myself in nature and my main focus was on planting trees and flowers.

The only time I found the urge to go out the house was when one of my childhood friends who had married an American came back home to sell her possessions and put her house up for sale. I went to help her with a garage sale she had organised but did not know where to start.

I noticed a bookshelf full of books and asked her what she intended to do with them. "Don't know" she said, "who would buy that rubbish, I never read them." They belonged to a 'crazy' old boyfriend that she had deliberately forgotten about.

As I fetched a box and started to put the books in, the whole contents of the bookshelf fell on top of me and scattered on the floor. Retrieving them one by one, I could not help noticing the titles: *The Third Eye* by Lobsang Rampa, *Psychic Discoveries behind the Iron Curtain*, *The Kirlian Aura*, *Linda Goodman's Star Signs*, and an array of books on mysticism. *Had these books been sitting on a shelf for years gathering dust, patiently waiting and now hurling themselves at me in their bid to embrace me?*

I bought the lot, grateful to have something to take to bed instead of a bottle.

With my new bed companions, I now managed much needed sleep, so deep that all went black and blank. Frankly, in contrast to the recent past, I would have preferred to stay awake all night and devour the information at a greater and faster rate, but I still needed the solace of the bush during the day.

My memories now interjected throughout the day.

I remembered when I was young and in love with life and music and dancing. I would sometimes dim the lights, lay back, and close my eyes listening to my favourite music. Through my closed eyes, a whole band would come to life, and I would watch a stage performance, the likes of which I had never seen, dancing to the music that was playing. I was particularly fond of ballet and Russian dancing, and the dancers delighted me with their self-expression, their agility, their costumes, right down to their sometimes unnecessarily garish make-up. The only disconcerting aspect of this show was the fact that the characters always floated in the air. Their feet never touched the ground. *But what the heck!*

It had never occurred to me to question the source of these visions. I had assumed they were the property of each one of us.

Later in life, as I became obsessed with clothes and set to become a dress designer, the visions changed to fashion parades. These usually took place on Balmoral Beach. The girls would always move from right to left, each following the other. An Italian Photographer (God only knows how I knew he was Italian) with shoulder length curly black hair, wearing a black vest and a white shirt with rolled-up sleeves that hugged his muscles and the sight of which made me go to pieces, would take pictures. Unfortunately, I never saw his entire face, try as I did. All I managed was a side view, as I would always be standing behind him to the left. He was divinely handsome.

As each girl approached him, I would hear a buzz followed by a click, and the girl would smile and freeze. She would then move on and the next girl would come forward. Sometimes they moved too fast for me to take in all the details of the garments they were wearing, but I had no control over the flow of their movements.

One day, one of the fabrics seemed so intriguing that I automatically stretched my arm and touched it, as it was my habit to do, in real life, whenever I wanted to get in touch with the feel of a fabric, to determine the shape it wanted to assume, before unfolding into a final design. Alarmed, I had to retract my hand automatically because the fabric was much rougher than I expected. It looked metallic and I thought it would be soft like glow-mesh, but it had the feel of rough metal. *Seeing was one thing, but touching a vision...!!!*

Don't ask me to offer you any explanation.

... *How I wished I could retrieve these lost faculties.*

~~~~~

RECALL 8

It never ceases to amaze me how often my extraordinary wishes are granted, yet I never get accustomed to the idea.

After a hard day of gardening I went to bed that night utterly exhausted. Anxiety had left my life but normality was never to revisit me.

Sleep evaded me but a dead calm descended on me as I closed my eyes. Very slowly and gently, a bud appeared at the top right corner of my closed eye and moved down and settled in front of my nose and proceeded to open up into the most glorious flower I had ever seen. This was followed by a procession of flowers the likes of which do not exist on planet Earth. The colours were unbelievably brilliant and out-worldly.

As each flower opened up, my heart opened a little until I dozed off into the most peaceful sleep I had had in months.

Next day a forgotten poem popped into my head and I remembered....

I remembered when at the age of 7 I asked my parents to transfer me to the French School in my neighbourhood, run by nuns. I had not yet been exposed to the tyranny of the Catholic religion. A few months into catechism classes I knew I was doomed to hell for eternity. There apparently was no salvation for the likes of me.

I had an ingenious idea to overcome the fear of eternal damnation: what if the head nun would allow me to attend the Koran classes instead, which were meant for the small number of Muslims attending the school. Fate would have it that one of the Muslim girls had her heart set on attending catechism classes. As I was a lost cause anyway, they allowed the swap in the hope of recruiting one of the others to their side. At least, that's what I figured.

That's when I developed a love for Arabic poetry, and I decided to attend Arabic classes which were optional for foreigners, and I was the only foreigner who took up the option, ever.

One particular segment of poetry stuck in my head and played out in my mind for years on end every time I took an extended shower. The words resonated in my head but their meaning, and certainly their purpose, had totally evaded me.

On this particular day, I decided to get to the bottom of this puzzle, so I dropped the shovel, jumped in the shower, sat on the floor, and waited for the words to play out in my head and, actually, listened to them for the first time in decades. I sat on the floor totally mesmerised by what I was hearing until the water went cold.

It was the most gut wrenching poetry I had ever heard, about a man seeking enlightenment and begging for the wisdom to break through the entrails of darkness to quench his thirst for knowledge. A Sufi teaching as I understand it now.

How or why would a 7 year old tomboy seek and hold on for years to a yearning for a kind of knowledge totally foreign to her and beyond her comprehension level?

... Tears were pouring down my face, but I was not crying.

~~~~~

RECALL 9

I also remembered another mantra that continuously played out in my head as a child, which seemed to be incongruously planted into my head.

It went like this:

There are those who have no capacity to learn to read or understand.
There are those who have no desire to learn to read or understand.
There are those who want to learn to read but have no capacity to understand.
There are those who read and understand but never make use of their knowledge.

There are those who read, understand, and make use of that knowledge. There are those who read, understand, make use of their knowledge and, in turn, write for others to read, understand, and gain knowledge.

This reminds me of the psychic my sister-in-law dragged me to. Apart from the Pope Joan insight I mentioned previously, she also announced: "You will be known for the word." "Which word?" I asked in all innocence. At that point in my life I had no inklings of ever becoming a writer as I had no concept of what I could be writing about.

I am not psychic, but I could clearly see what went on in her head. She thought this was the most pathetic prediction she had ever made and it was time for her to quit before she ruined her reputation beyond repair.

But do you see a pattern here?

Was life doggedly conspiring to make a writer out of me by drumming into my head ideas that I was not equipped to bring forth? True, I was very good at creative writing at school. In fact, I was good at every subject except history, which made no sense to me, but none of that amounted to anything at the end.

Knowledge? What knowledge? I couldn't even run my own life successfully. How could I expect anyone to take me seriously when my life was such a mess?

And if I told anyone about the things that were happening now, they would certainly lock me up.

That would certainly suit my husband who was by now bent on taking everything away from me, making me bankrupt, and declaring me insane. He actually openly told me so and was actively seeking ways to actualise his plan,

... "So I am not telling anyone", I thought to myself.

~~~~

RECALL 10

Nothing remains hidden forever. Secrets have a way of exposing themselves when you least expect them to and in the most insidious manner.

We were putting the final touches to the swimming pool so we could put the house up for sale as my husband transferred our business to his personal name, stopped paying all bills as well as the mortgage, and our liability escalated to $250,000 in a matter of months. The bank was foreclosing on us.

Cash had become a rare commodity, and I was making do whichever way I could. My husband wanted to pave the path to the pool with pebbles. I thought that would be hard to walk on with bare feet and it was something we could not afford, being so deep into debt. I had an old box of grass seeds which I thought I would plant. He said they were too old to take, the soil was clay, the area shaded, so there was no way the grass would grow. I said let's try. He said no chance. I said I believe in miracles. He gave me 2 weeks.

I planted the seeds and watered them feverishly every day. Two weeks passed: no sign of grass. He said he was getting the pebbles the next day. Forlorn, I made my way to the pool and to my complete amazement the grass had actually grown 2 inches. I ran upstairs calling my husband to say the grass had grown. "It can't have" he said. "I just came up from the pool there was no grass." I said "I just saw it 2 minutes ago." "I am not going all the way down; I know there is no grass there" he objected. I managed to drag him down.

To my horror, the grass had disappeared. He thought I was playing games. I assured him I had seen grass with my own eyes and I picked up a dead twig and drew 3 circles where I had seen bare patches because of heavy clay in these particular spots; the rest had been covered in lush green grass. He mumbled under his breath and rushed upstairs.

A week passed and somehow he had forgotten about the pebbles.

I had not dared venture to the pool area since the incident. I can't remember why I had to go down, but there was the elusive grass again in lush green with the same 3 bare patches. Should I call him and show him? What if the grass disappeared again? I turned my back on the grass, counted to 10 and turned around and the grass was still there. I still had my doubts but I summoned enough courage to drag him down once again.

This time the grass had stayed put and the 3 bare patches I had circled previously stood out in their glorious nakedness as though to bear testimony to my previous sighting of an invisible phenomenon.

Had it not been for these 3 bare patches I had so staunchly circled, the whole episode could have been explained away as wishful thinking.

Don't ask me for an explanation.

... "There are more things in Heaven and Earth, Horatio" - Shakespeare.

~~~~~

RECALL 11

That was the beginning of a string of occurrences that led my husband to call me a witch.

A new identity for my clean slate?

Perhaps an old identity resurfacing.

Though history is something my mind refuses to grasp, a segment of history evokes in me revulsion, repulsion, and deep sorrow at mankind's inhumanity, and that is the period of the Inquisition that spanned over 600 years and ended only 200 years ago.

The Inquisition was a campaign of torture, mutilation, mass murder, and destruction of human life perpetrated by "The Supreme Sacred Congregation of the Holy Office of the Roman Catholic Church," which is the most highly regarded institution on the planet. This time was the darkest period in recent history which ran parallel and concurrently with the Age of Enlightenment of the Renaissance and in the same region.

How could that happen? How could the 2 extremes live side by side? It somehow reminded me of the contrast between my inner and outer life that I was undergoing.

I wondered if I had been accused of being a witch, perhaps tortured and even burnt at the stake in a past life?

That could explain why when I watch re-enactments of that period I feel a total identification with the horror and find myself drawn into the emotions of the scenes as though living them in the present; whereas, when I watch other periods, I can maintain my status as observer while still feeling empathy for the other.

That would also explain why Napoleon stood out as my hero in school. Perhaps my allegiance to him dated back to the time he delivered the world from the tyranny of the Inquisition, not to mention his many other conquests and achievements, depending on which history book you read.

Reincarnation was a theme that was central to all the books I was reading. The more I thought about it, the more it served to explain things that were otherwise impossible to explain, regarding my personal life.

But what was even more interesting is that when I detached myself from my personal story and viewed life objectively, everything appeared different, and the meaning I attached to events lost their purpose and their hold over me.

A totally new set of questions were popping into my head.

What if reincarnation was real?

It would explain something that had intrigued me all along: how come my son was born with a fully formed strong character from day one of his birth and could undeniably communicate his wishes, likes and dislikes, so effectively? He was an avid learner from a young age and whenever I taught him anything, he grasped it straight away as though my teachings were serving simply as reminders.

I remembered this being the case with me when I was at school. When the teacher explained a new concept, the silent response in my head was usually "of course." This seems to be an ability one loses as one gets older; perhaps the general consensus of opinion takes hold and paves the way for conditioning and indoctrination.

Reincarnation could also explain justice as life viewed from a single lifetime's perspective seems senseless, futile, and often unjust. People who lead lives of crime and cruelty often are rewarded with riches and privileges, while others, through seemingly no fault of their own, are born, live, and die in misery. We can find solace in the idea of eternal damnation or rewards in paradise according to one's deeds and misdeeds but how do you explain away the seemingly random conditions into which we are each born?

The greatest let down of all is the supposed attainment of wisdom on your death bed when it no longer serves you. What's the point? Would a Universe that has created every single thing or life form with its own intrinsic purpose and usefulness, have endowed its masterpiece "Man" with the most haphazard and inane existence?

Who is the joke on?

While I began this inner treasure hunt for answers, my world on the outside was being stripped to the bone.

... How I wished I could extricate myself from my outer world of utter chaos and plunge wholeheartedly into this inner space of wonder and discovery.

~~~~~

RECALL 12

It was becoming a matter of course that these deeper wishes emanating from the recesses of my heart were being granted speedily and were landing in my lap without me even knowing which way to turn to get them.

Most of the time I didn't even realise that I was asking or even what I was asking for precisely. These were happening on a subconscious level. What was at the very back of my mind and deep in my heart was so enormous and intangible that I couldn't even begin to conceptualise them. Even miracles couldn't hold such power.

I don't remember asking for anything tangible at the time, as the amount of debt accumulated and other losses were so far beyond my ability to start the rebuilding process that I simply put the whole sordid affair out of my mind so "I" wouldn't go out of my mind." There simply was not enough room in my mind for both me and the problems. There was just enough room for me and my son that I loved and cherished beyond any concept of love I had ever held.

All else could go to hell, but WE were heading for paradise ... *somehow.*

As it happened, the next day my son called out to me to watch a program on TV in which he thought I would be interested. This was my first introduction to the Oprah Winfrey show. Daytime shows had never caught my fancy but this was different; Oprah was interviewing Deepak Chopra. I was hooked. I knew then and there that the door to my salvation was opening up. Deepak happened to be in Australia that week and was conducting a seminar at the Convention Centre. We had no money to eat, but who cared about food when mana from heaven was being offered in lieu.

I made it to the seminar.

The morning session brought a whole new set of insights into my head, and I was energised like I hadn't been for a very long time. By late afternoon, I was giddy and must have slipped into a state which I can only call a trance. This was the first time I had such an experience.

The lighting on the stage seemed to change to a much softer hue. Deepak's voice got more and more distant as he receded from my perception and began to fade. My eyes narrowed and focused on this person who was now becoming so familiar to me that I was seized with an obsession to know who he was. I knew him. I knew him so well. I knew him inside out.

I was conscious of the fact that the only other time I had heard of him or seen him was on the Oprah show. Another part of me kept asking doggedly: "I know him, I've always known him, I know him intimately, *but who is he?*"

And the bewildering answer popped into my head: "HE IS ME!!!"

What a preposterous thought!

Yet the sense of identification was complete and overwhelming.

Could a part of me have perceived the future me integrating with Deepak's then mindset - his matrix of reality?

Much later, I was introduced to the concept of soul groups. Is it at all possible that I do belong to Deepak's Soul group at some level? Could that other part of me have known and recognised this, ahead of me, and intruded on my conscious awareness?

Nothing though could have been further from my mind than the possibility that one day I too would be writing about the same things. Could this have been a precognition which I failed to recognise at the time?

... I was on the road to recovery: recovery of long lost knowledge.

~~~~

RECALL 13

I had been for some time submerging myself in the study of the books that literally fell over my head and all my spare time was devoted to putting into practice what I was learning. I even discovered a section in the local library dedicated to the occult and the supernatural – thankfully for free.

The natural in my life had no appeal. It spelt "suffering." The fact that my exercises were not yielding any tangible results at that point was of no consequence; at least, they were diverting my focus away from my misery and the hopelessness of my life situation.

I could appease my mind with my books and hold my emotions at bay with my new discoveries. Still, money was a most persistent and pressing problem that lurked at the back of my mind and drove me to distraction.

Blissfully, I came across a book eulogising the power of mantras. Reciting mantras to yourself was supposed to change your life and open up new possibilities. Having no better alternative at hand, I decided to move the money problem from the back of my mind to the forefront of my thoughts and tackle it head on.

Most of the mantras supplied went against the grain and raised objections in my head. I decided to design my very own, tailor-made to my personality and my dire need of the moment. Stripped to the absolute point, it went like this:

Money now comes to me from all directions, freely, easily, abundantly.

I recited this mantra religiously and without fail, in bed, in the shower, in the car, in the garden, at the kitchen sink.

Frankly, I did not expect anything to come out of it, but at least it was driving any unpleasant thoughts that were sneaking into my head OUT!!!

I was rewarded with the most incredible dream. In my dream, I was in Paris, in a shoddy little cafe with red and white checked table clothes. I was with a tall man, 6'2, incredibly handsome, with piercing blue eyes, masses of blond curls, a soft face, and of German origin. He was wearing faded blue jeans and a white muslin shirt unbuttoned to the waist. We were sharing a bottle of Chianti and a loaf of Italian bread. He poured the wine into 2 cheap wine glasses, broke the bread into 2 pieces, gave me half, raised his glass and said "You will never go hungry again."

Though the man in my dream resembled in no way any image of Christ I could have possibly carried in my mind, and despite the fact that I had stopped praying a very long time ago, upon waking I was convinced this was Jesus. I was convinced this was no ordinary dream, and I was convinced that what He meant was that all of my financial problems would be over ... *for good...*

... but why German?

... A sense of peace and optimism engulfed my being. I was reinstated to Cloud 9.

~~~~~

RECALL 14

Things were happening so fast now I lost all sense of time or sequence of events. The supernatural was overtaking the natural and the nature of my reality was turning on its axis.

Even in retrospect, I can't fathom how my financial situation overturned and how fast it all happened, without any planning or much help on my part, and often in the most ridiculous or embarrassingly delightful ways. But I wasn't complaining. In fact, I was now care-free and deliriously happy.

My problems? What problems? They were no longer mine; I delegated them to my newly found Universe whose powers were apparently much greater than mine.

The people in my life that I so loved and trusted, and who finally betrayed me to the core, fell out of my life and left a large gap that I could now fill whichever way I pleased.

I threw myself wholeheartedly into this new world of mine: the supernatural, which proved itself to be by far **"The Super(ior Form of the) Natural."**

At first, these manifested in small ways.

At the supermarket, my son had picked a few items which were not absolutely vital to our subsistence. Putting my emotions aside, I explained that I did not have enough money on me and I promised that at the first opportunity I would buy him these items. Without resistance or complaint, he put them back on the shelf.

At the check-out, I had a strong urge to crawl under the counter. Embarrassing as this was, I succumbed to the urge, and there laid a crisp $20 note waiting for me to fulfil my promise to my son. I did not know the rightful owner of it, so I accepted it as a gift from the Universe.

Not long after, we went to the bookshop to buy him school books that he needed. I bought what I could afford but was one book short. My son fretted over going back to school without all of the required books. Again, I made a solemn promise that I would get it for him in time, without any idea where the money would come from. And again, as I stepped out of the doors of the bookshop, my foot landed on a $20 note. This was the exact amount I needed to add to the change left in my purse to purchase the much needed book.

Another time, my son confided that he was down to his last $6.00 and desperately needed $1,000 for various school and personal requirements. How could I promise that I would get him "one thousand dollars"? Instead I said "You know, the Universe will provide." "Fat chance" whispered the cynic in my ear.

When we checked the mail a couple of days later, there was a letter for my son. "Is this really for me? Who would write to me?" he asked. I said,

"Open it and find out." Inside was a cheque for $1,000.00 made out to my son as an unsolicited scholarship from a firm of solicitors that years later he ended up working for. This was long, long before he ever thought of becoming a lawyer.

These miracles were now taking place with such monotonous regularity and the money and opportunities to make money were manifesting so easily, without any rhyme or reason, apparently out of thin air, that I lost all emotional charge associated with money and, therefore, I have very little recall of how the little threads of it all wove themselves into a new tapestry of abundance for my life.

As I write this I am looking at a collection of a $100 & two $20 notes that the wind blew up my skirt and literally into my hands, on a calm afternoon walking home from the beach, and which I have framed as a constant reminder that money flies to me on the wings of the wind.

... Had I accessed the source of the perpetual windfall ?

~~~~~

RECALL 15

Now that I had established this unshakable connection to the source that would gratify my every financial need, I marvelled at the ease with which I had been able to put all my trust in this invisible means of support.

The bills kept coming and the debts were accumulating, but I had this unshakable faith that all would be well and that these would all be taken care of as and when they fell due. Some days I was hanging by the skin of my teeth, but my mouth kept smiling exposing those strong teeth to the world, in defiance to the illusions of the natural world.

They say your inner world is reflected in your outer world. Nothing could have been further from the truth at that time. In fact, my inner world operated in total contrast to my outer world.

Much as I trusted this invisible, intangible, incomprehensible inner world of mine, trust in my outer circumstances was a major issue for me.

I was receiving many conflicting reports from friends, anonymous phone calls, and especially from my husband whose erratic behaviour riddled my life with doubt. He would shun me then plead with me. He would threaten me then cry for me not to leave. He would blame me for pushing him away; yet, deny that he was being unfaithful. He maintained that his relationship with the other woman was purely of a business nature and that he was working hard to support "his family."

What was most confusing was that he no longer created opportunities for fights so he could storm out with a legitimate excuse to stay away, without having to cover up his clandestine encounters with his girlfriend who had by now left her husband for mine.

Yet, more than ever, I could not trust him. The accusations mounted and the guilt I felt for the possibility that I may be doing him an injustice with "my insane jealousy" was too much to bear. I had no proof, just a hunch.

I needed proof but hiring a private investigator was out of my league. I simply needed to know, one way or the other, so I could forge a direction for my life without regrets. But it was not simple. A lifetime of doubts ahead of me was simply insupportable.

I spent the whole night conjuring up ways that would lead me to the truth. At 4:00 a.m., exhausted, I fell asleep. At 7:15 a.m., I received a phone call from a stranger saying he was walking his dog and came across a parcel that his dog was about to pee on, which contained business documents with a name and this telephone number, and he asked if I knew the person. I said that was my husband but he was away on business interstate for a couple of weeks. He suggested I go and pick up the parcel. I said I would after I had dropped my son off to school.

The stranger lived a couple of suburbs away and a quick glance at the contents of the envelope revealed bank statements, cheque butts, and receipts for cash he had received from a business he was now conducting with his new partner/girlfriend.

Feeling overwhelmed that he was telling me the truth, I shoved the contents back in the envelope....

.... but a small envelope, with a piece torn and exposing a handwriting I thought I recognised, fell to the floor.

The envelope was addressed to my husband c/o his girlfriend to an address interstate. It was a letter from his sister in England congratulating him for moving in with his girlfriend and was wondering when he would be announcing the lucky day: their wedding.

The mystery was revealed, my questions answered, my need gratified.

Within the space of 5 minutes my overwhelming feeling had escalated to rage and dissolved into peace.

The truth sets you free.

And I was free. Free of doubt. Free of guilt. Free of fear.

Free to live life on my terms.

*... **Free to dream up new reality pictures.***

~~~~~

RECALL 16

Freedom would have to be one of the top priorities on anyone's dream list; yet, one of the most elusive.

For the individual seeking freedom, the prospects are grim. One has to face up to a great deal of loss: loss of many privileges that come with the approval of peers and society, loss of that sense of belonging, co-operation and co-dependence that humans crave; and have to subsequently endure rejection, ridicule, isolation, and loneliness.

Society rejects freedom because of the fear of losing control. They imagine that the individual seeking freedom will indulge in excesses, kill and pillage, and seek only individual gratification with total disregard for the welfare of others.

What loved ones, family and friends, fear is that the freedom seeker will no longer be slave to their demands and expectations, silent as these may often be.

Well apart from the personal internal demons created by one's past conditioning, the individual has to contend with the obstacles presented by the whole of society and their peers.

They all impose their laws, their rules, their regulations, and their conditions.

Though I have a most loving and supportive small (very small) family, I did not escape the tyranny of such impositions. "What will people say?" was a question that evoked murderous tendencies within the core of my being. "They can all go to hell," I thought. "Not I."

Friends, with the best of intentions, whispered with authority: "If you are clever, you can win him back, you know."

"Win him back?" What a hideous thought, why would I want to win a treacherous liar? If anything, I wanted to lose him … *fast*.

I had in fact previously called the girlfriend with precisely that notion in mind. That was the one and only phone call I had ever made to her. She did not pick up; I left a message. She called back. Unbeknownst to me, she and my husband were recording the conversation, thinking my motive behind the call was to threaten her.

What I said was: "You and I have something in common in my husband. You want him and I want to get rid of him, both of us are failing. Perhaps, if we joined forces I could teach you how to win him over and you could teach me how to lose him, and we can both succeed." All she said was, "This conversation is not leading anywhere" and hung up.

I learnt later that she had burst into tears and was so upset, she literally fainted. Fainting was a convenience she was graced with that made Knights in Shining Armour gallop to her rescue. My husband cherished that role; it made him feel strong, needed, and like a hero. Modern women have lost that nous.

The consensus of opinion remained steadfast. I had to win my husband back so I could claim victory and regain the love and approval of others and my own self-respect, all in one coup. The love extended with these well intended morsels of advice made me nauseous and caused me anguish beyond the limits of my ability to bear and in one of these memorable sessions, I blurted out with meticulous conviction *"whoever stays with him will end up with cancer, and it ain't gonna be me."*

My words stunned me as much as the others. A dead silence fell upon us.

This was not something I had consciously thought of, but...

... At that moment I was in tune with the Laws of the Universe.

~~~~~

RECALL 17

Was this a prophesy?
Was this a premonition?
Was this wishful thinking on my part?
Was this a curse I placed on her? After all, I was supposed to be a witch!

Let me take you back to a period of my life when I suffered severe migraines. These started at the tender age of 12. I had periods of years when I had these excruciating migraines. They then disappeared for years. They would again come back and disappear once again without any rhyme or reason.

At the age of 29, after a debilitating session which had lasted 3 days, I went to my doctor, a very rare thing for me to do except for a prescription of The Pill. My doctor cheerfully greeted me with, "How are you today Mrs …?" to which I ungraciously responded, "Would I be here if I was well?"

My doctor was in fact an angel but, despite his unscrupulous honesty, he possessed no miraculous powers. He very openly confessed that doctors did not know what caused migraines. They thought it was food related, mostly chocolate, coffee, or even oranges. I could find out through a process of elimination, he suggested but alas there was no known cure yet. He then prescribed some very expensive tablets that I could take at the onset of a migraine if I was seeking a placebo effect but that, to his knowledge, they never really worked.

Very reluctantly, I tried one, thus counteracting the placebo effect. Justly, in accordance with my negative expectations, it proved to be useless.

This was a defining moment in my life: I had to absolutely *define* what was the root cause of this ailment. Analysing the history of my diet, I quickly determined it had nothing to do with food. I was then back to square one not knowing where to start.

It occurred to me to map out the periods when I had the migraines, and the periods when they disappeared, to uncover what a 12 year old had in common with a 29 year old. "Immaturity" immediately sprang to mind. Emotionally, I was stuck on 12 and did not want to budge.

That aside, I had to work this out scientifically. I remembered distinctly that my migraines started at 12 and stopped at 17. They started again at 20 and stopped at 22 and started again when I got married to the day of my scientific investigation.

What-was-the-common-denominator in my life during the periods of intense migraines? I asked intently, deliberately, and very slowly, narrowing my eyes and grasping for an answer. Instantly the word "Dominator" struck me between the eyes. During these periods my life was "dominated" by 3 different men, stopping me from following the direction of my life.

The first was my older brother, who is 7 years older, who took it upon himself to groom me to society's expectations, which was the Egyptian code of behaviour. I was no longer allowed to climb trees or do all the boyish things I always craved. On the other hand, I had to hide any hint of my burgeoning femininity. A prison was installed in my head and the walls were too close together to allow any movement forward, any sense of individuality, any freedom. When I hit 17, my brother took off to Brazil in search of his own freedom, the walls of my prison crumbled, and I was set free. No more migraines.

At 20, I migrated to Australia with my younger brother. A very kind friend of the family, around the same age as my older brother, offered us accommodation and took it upon himself to take over where my brother left off. One of the restrictions was that I was not allowed to make friends with Australians so I would not risk corruption. The migraines revisited with vengeance.

My younger brother and I had no money to start out on our own, and it took a year and a half to save enough to set ourselves up. The day we moved out, the migraines ceased miraculously.

I married an Australian, and though my husband was not controlling, the direction he wanted to take in his life was diametrically opposed to mine, and as the good little girl I was, I abandoned mine and followed his. Migraines became once again a predictable part of my life ….

…. until this moment of realisation. I could now feel the tension discharge from my head, move down my neck and back, onto my shoulders, arms and drain though my fingers. My body went limp and a delicious wave of relaxation cleansed my body, my mind, and my soul.

I vowed I would never let another man dictate my destiny. I vowed I would now take complete control of the direction of my life. I packed up my bags and left. The migraines were now past history.

The mistake I made was that I associated migraines with control by men. Sometimes we, women, get controlled by other women but we don't recognise it or label it as such. This has happened only twice since the vow I made to myself. The migraines hit me to alert me of the situation. The minute I recognised the event for what it was and promised myself to get myself out of the situation and not allow myself back there, the migraines subsided within minutes.

I now don't have to suffer or get rid of people; I just put myself back in control of the situation and the direction of my life. "No" has become the most positive word in my vocabulary. It's the cure for migraines.

... I was connecting the dots.

~~~~

RECALL 18

Another clue to my ominous "prediction" in Recall 16, where I associated a mindset with a disease, was an incident which had taken place a few months before.

As I mentioned previously, a couple of my closest friends were actively participating in the destruction of my marriage. This was something I would have never believed in a million years as I trusted them implicitly with the deepest secrets of my soul.

Naïve, trusting, ignorant, blind, and stupid were synonyms that described me to a tee.

One friend in particular, Zelda, had provided accommodation in her house to my husband's girlfriend so he could carry on with her. Her malice extended to the point of befriending my brother and using him to extract from him information about me and to feed him false information to act on. She used the ruse "I am telling you this for her own good, but I want you to promise me not to repeat to her all of what I am telling you." Only selective disinformation he was allowed to relay.

This situation drove me to the brink of insanity. My brother would advise me to take certain actions which were contrary to my gut feeling, with the notion that he knew better because of the information provided by my 'best friend,' but that he could not divulge because he had given his word that he wouldn't repeat them.

This was the workings of a master manipulator, feeding my mind with venomous thoughts yet rendering me impotent to make any lucid decisions by keeping me in the dark.

I did not get migraines. Instead, that was when I was vomiting blood.

One night, when my guts were churning out, I decided to ring Zelda and ask her why she wouldn't talk to me, yet send advice through my brother. She replied: "I just want him to do the right thing by Her" (meaning the girlfriend, someone she had only met a few months earlier). This didn't make sense.

"What about me?" I asked. She chuckled and said, "That's because he doesn't love you." I reminded her of the extent I had put myself out to successfully bring her husband back to her when he was being unfaithful to her, by showing him the error of his ways. "Oh," she said dismissively. "You are perfect and I am not."

For the first time in our friendship, I detected the venom in her voice. Jealousy had been eating away at her, and I had never ever suspected it.

I spent another sleepless night, tossing and turning, wondering how I would put an end to this nightmare.

In the morning, I had the answer.

I met my brother, and I asked him if he would be prepared to grant me the same favour he granted Zelda. "Of course," was his response. "I want you to promise me that you will never ever talk to Zelda about me again. And you will never ever mention her name to me or act on her 'caring and helpful' advice regarding me."

"If that's what you want, it's easily done," he said.

"And you will see," I added, "that as I close this door and erect this brick wall between us, when she can no longer spew her venom at me, where will it go? I bet it turns inwards and destroys her guts."

I had effectively put an abrupt stop to the messages.

Within days, I had recovered my health. Within 3 months she was in hospital having part of her guts removed.

Was this a prophesy?
Was this a premonition?
Was this wishful thinking on my part?
Was this a curse I placed on her?

The reality is, our thinking creates emotions, and emotions affect the chemistry of our body, and venomous thinking creates venomous emotions which can be projected onto others contributing to their destruction or turned inwards, destroying ourselves.

So long as I remained open to her venomous intentions and invested my emotions into them, my life was crumbling and I was being sick. Once I had made the decision not to accept them into my reality, her venom had nowhere to go except turn on herself and destroy her. That is also what is known as karma. What you put out will come back to you.

In that moment, a new awareness had dawned on me. It is not what other people do to you; it is what you allow into your mind, into your heart, and into your life.

34

Zelda was no longer relevant to my life, just a model not to emulate and to keep at arm's length. She did what she did because of her own unhappiness, and that served me as a great lesson.

She taught me clarity of mind, to see others for what they truly are and not how I want them to be.
She taught me emotional independence by not getting drawn into other people's insecurities.
She taught me that people do evil things not because they are evil but because they are thoroughly unhappy.
She taught me that people's perception of you is coloured by their perception of themselves and their own self-images.
She taught me that your life circumstances are a projection of your own thinking and, more importantly, the thinking of others that you take upon yourself.
She taught me independence of mind, emotion, and action.
She taught me detachment from my story and writing a new script for my life.

You can imagine how grateful I was when several months later, I came across a little blue book by Louise Hay called, *"Heal your Body"* in which she describes this very mind/body connection through emotional patterns that I had independently come to realise.

This book relieved me of any guilt I might have felt years later when "my husband's girlfriend" got cancer. She chose to stay in a potentially destructive relationship.

... I opted for a life of magic and miracles.

~~~~~

RECALL 19

The house had been on the market for several months now, and we were getting dangerously close to the date the bank had set for foreclosure. It was a most beautiful house, architect designed, and picturesque. We brought the price down considerably, but there were still no takers.

With my newly found awareness, I now realised it was my attachment to the house, despite its unsavoury memories, that kept the buyers at bay. I decided it was time to let go and let the Universe take over, as by now I was convinced I could create an even better life for myself, despite all outward appearances to the contrary.

With this in mind, I made a list of all the properties on the market corresponding to the sum that would be left after paying the enormous debts we had accumulated.

Et voila! A buyer appeared out of the blue keen to exchange contracts rapidly. We couldn't let our one and only chance of avoiding foreclosure and ruination go. We exchanged.

The properties I was inspecting turned out to be hell holes, not resembling the slightest bit the beautiful picture I had created in my mind for my next home. I added another $150,000 to the price bracket I envisaged. Still hell holes.

What was absolutely insane was the fact that I was looking for properties with our combined share of the proceeds of the sale of the house, despite the fact that I had no intention of resuming a relationship with my husband, and despite my husband's resolute assertions that he was bent on ruining me. For the life of me, I could not comprehend his intense need for revenge when he was the one to betray me; therefore, I figured it was best left unexplored.

There simply were no properties that my imagination could fathom living in, with half the money that would be my share, not even a bachelor unit. I had a son to accommodate. What was even worse was that I was in no position to borrow without having a job and with the negative credit rating we had acquired.

But I persevered without any rhyme or reason, just out of a compulsion to do so.

I had a dream, in black and white.

In my dream I was a man – a general in the army, my husband was a sergeant, we were in the trenches, but there was a ceasefire. The young soldier approached me with tears running down his face saying "I have to go home."

The next morning, I saw my husband leaning over the balustrade of one of the upper levels with tears running down his face. "I have to go home," he softly managed; an eerie echo of my dream.

"Home?" I asked. "I thought this is your home." "I have to go to England; my mother has died," he explained.

That afternoon he flew out.

I continued looking for a house, way out of my league even with our combined share of the property. I looked at 45 houses with nothing that matched the picture in my mind. I kept repeating to each real estate agent "I want a brand new house, 3-4 bedrooms, with all the rooms off a central courtyard." Every real estate agent would look at me incredulously and say, "You will never get that here; you will have to move interstate for that and even if you got one, you would have to pay over a million dollars for it."

My mind was made up, and it wouldn't budge.

A couple of weeks later, I had another dream in black and white.

I was standing on the platform of a train station with 2 suitcases packed up. I was waiting for a train – destination unknown.

If a train symbolises destination as well as a train of thought, my thoughts, too, lacked any logical or clear direction to follow.

It was now Monday, and we had to be out of the house by Saturday morning as settlement would take place on Friday at 5:00 p.m.

A month had passed, and there had been no word from my husband. I started the laborious task of packing up.

On Wednesday morning, I made a booking with the removalist and asked for a quote. He asked for details of items to be moved (2 truckloads – *2 suitcases?*) and my address. He then asked for the address I was moving to. "I don't know," I said. "What do you mean I don't know," he asked, bewildered. "It means: I wouldn't have a clue," I said. "Lady," he said, "in my 30 years in this business I've never come across anyone who made a booking to move and didn't know where they were going. How can I give you a quote, and what will we do with your stuff once we load it up?"

"Give me a quote for a 10km radius and on Saturday morning I may have your answer," I said. Was this also an echo of my most recent dream that still lingered in my head? Destination unknown!

… Magic was what I wanted for my life. A Miracle is what was needed.

~~~~~

RECALL 20

On Wednesday, just after booking the removalist in, a friend of mine, whom I had lost touch with, rang me out of the blue and asked how things were going.

Within 5 minutes she had regretted asking the question, as I launched into a tirade of the latest happenings of my life.

"Have you looked at Seaforth?" she asked, taking control of the situation. "I am not living in Woop Woop!" I asserted, noting that the humiliating experiences of the previous couple of years had not exerted the slightest influence on my grandiose dreams and how I envisioned myself and my life in the future.

"Don't be so bloody closed-minded," she snapped. "Get your street directory out and take a look. It's only 5 minutes away, across the bridge, from where you're looking," and she hung up in disgust before wasting any more of her precious breath on a nincompoop.

I jumped in the car and stubbornly headed in the opposite direction to Seaforth but not before looking it up in the street directory as my friend suggested. As I had already compassed all the real estate agents within a 10km radius, I drove right out of the territory of my choice and stumbled upon a small realtor tucked away in a back street.

I repeated my well-rehearsed mantra: "I am looking for a brand new house, 3-4 bedrooms, with all the rooms off a central courtyard..." I didn't leave out the pitiful amount I had allocated for the property.

As expected, he started saying, "Well sorry, but you will never ...." He suddenly stopped, scratched his head, and said, "Hang on a minute. If I remember correctly, about 3 months ago we listed a property that sounds very much like what you're describing, but I didn't bother with it because it sounded weird. It is not the kind of property we deal with in this area, you know. It's a very strange and unique set-up. Although it's a house, it's a dual occupancy title, and I don't know how the council has passed it because it has very little land and everybody around here wants a large block of land. It is built in the backyard of an existing property but is totally self-contained with its own entrance and garage."

"Nuh," he said. "You won't want to see it. It's not even in this area. It's way out..." "Where is it?" I interrupted suspiciously, narrowing my eyes. "Seaforth," he said. "Do you know Seaforth?"

SEAFORTH! (or SEE FORTH? A pun intended by the Universe?) Bells were ringing in my head.

"That's the one," I said. "That's my house. Take me there at once," and I dragged him out of the office before he could protest or put his coat on.

I took one step inside the house, and I couldn't believe my eyes. It matched perfectly the picture in my mind. A brand new house, with all the latest stainless steel appliances, and all the main rooms off a central courtyard. It looked like a small corner of paradise, and it was more than what I could wish for.

Was I dreaming? Was this magic or a miracle?

"I want it," I announced. "Let me speak to the builder," he said. "No", I said. "There is no time; give me his number, and I'll speak to him." "I can't do that," he objected. "Who says?" I asked. We drove back to his office, and I got the number off him. The builder did not answer his phone.

Thursday morning my husband walked in the door exhausted and dazed.

Obliterating from my memory and perception what had come to pass the last couple of years, I rang the builder, made an appointment to view the property, and dragged my husband to the scene of my dreams. His eyes lit up at the sight of the house, then glazed over once again. We went back home, and he virtually passed out.

I spent Friday negotiating a price with the builder, despite the fact that this property was listed for half its value had it been standing on its own land. He said he had an offer for $25,000 more than what I was offering. I said, in my opinion, the property was worth a heck of a lot more than what he was asking for, but the fact of the matter was that I only had so much money I could spare.

I could give him a cheque for the full amount at 5:00 p.m. on the dot, without fiddling around with bank finance or waiting for his other prospect to make up her mind, which mightn't even eventuate. Before you know it, the $25,000 will be frittered in interest payments on finance, and other finishing touches which the other buyer would probably request and which I was prepared to relinquish, I argued.

"I want to move in tomorrow morning," I declared.

"What?" he cried out exhibiting signs of a heart attack. "Tomorrow morning? You need building and pest inspection reports, council certificates. These usually take 6 weeks."

"I'll move in under license," I said. "I don't know quite what that means but that's what we'll do; the solicitors will work it out. I have no choice, you see. We're settling on our property this afternoon. I have to move out tomorrow morning, and I have nowhere to go."

"That's not how things are done," he argued. "Who cares? If we agree to do it that way, then that's how they're done," I pleaded.

Exhausted with my unreasonable reasoning he gave me his solicitor's number and marched out saying, "Sort it out with him and get him to give me call," smugly relying on his solicitor to put me off.

Fat chance of that! I was pitifully desperate, and desperate situations call for desperate measures. I was so determined to hang on to my dream, lest I crumbled, that it didn't even occur to me that my husband would have other plans for his share of the money.

How everything was slotting into place was insane.

... If this was insanity, why do people opt for sanity? I wondered.

~~~~~

RECALL 21

Sanity is overrated. I have the proof.

Friday 3:30 p.m., I was on to my solicitor who was handling my divorce to exchange contracts on my new home in Seaforth. Surprisingly, he specialised in both matters.

"I can't possibly do that," he argued. "We need council certificates, building inspections, and pest inspections. I am advising you against that." He didn't even bother to mention the impending divorce, in total disdain for the obvious, though I could hear it on his mind.

"I am not ringing you for advice," I said firmly. "I AM INSTRUCTING YOU to exchange at 5:00 p.m. and draw up contracts to move under licence and pay rent, if necessary."

My husband walked in on me as I was having this heated discussion with my solicitor. "You're crazy," he said, "if you think you can organise all this by 5:00 p.m. You're dreaming."

Now the real crazy thing in this conversation was that it didn't occur to him to protest about buying this house jointly, considering we were heading for divorce.

At 5:00 p.m. on the dot, we were at the solicitor's signing contracts. I was sighing with relief, my husband was sighing with bewilderment, and my solicitor was sighing with total disapproval.

On Saturday morning, I did, indeed, have an address to which the removalist would move us.

I spent the whole weekend unpacking with resolve; yet, expecting at any moment to wake up and find it was all a dream.

Dreams, daydreams, and waking life overlapped and intruded on each other, and my sense of reality had changed permanently.

Within days and without preliminaries, my husband moved out.

He set up his office in one of the spare rooms of the new house. He would come at 7:30 a.m. to drive our son to school, something he rarely did before, return and work in his new home-office all day, then pick up our son and bring him home and leave after 8:30 p.m. to go to his bachelor pad.

We rarely talked during the day, but I cooked, and he joined us for dinner. I also paid all the bills from then on. Somehow, as promised, the Universe kept on providing.

I never asked for his motives for such an unusual arrangement. I hardly had the right to object when he had invested his share of the money in the current property.

I even looked forward to his trips interstate, supposedly on business, so I could immerse myself in my new ways without intrusion. If he was going there to see his girlfriend, that was his business.

Though we often shared the same physical space, in my mind and in my heart, he no longer occupied any space. I allowed him total freedom to conduct his life the way that suited him and, to maintain balance in my life, I allowed myself exactly the same privilege.

I had stumbled on the formula for detachment by suspending my judgement for his behaviour and had consequently reduced suffering to redundancy status.

Coinciding with the move to our new environment, I had fallen into new patterns of thinking, feeling, and behaving, and these patterns were now second nature to me, unfolding without any effort or will power.

I did away with worrying, as worrying never seemed to solve a problem.

I divorced myself from anything that didn't concern me, as these were futile to my life.

I no longer had any emotions invested in outcomes, as this saved disappointment.

What others did or thought were of no consequence to me, as they no longer had power over my life.

Enough money and opportunities presented themselves to me as and when needed, as I had transferred my trust to my invisible means of support.

Obstacles were my opportunity to practice my blossoming magic, as I delved into this and reaped the rewards.

When things seemed impossible, I saw them as the perfect time to expect a miracle, as life reflected that experience.

I laughed my problems away, as the Gods smiled on me.

My new way of being enchanted me, as I played the game of life.

Segregating myself from my outer reality and turning inwards had taken me from the roller coaster of my existence to a place of serenity and inner knowing that all was well in my world, as the riches of the inner world extended in front of me to eternity.

From agony to ecstasy, 2 years had elapsed.

... At what point did I come to land into this blissful state? I marvelled.

~~~~~

PART II

Conscious Creation

EPISODE 1

Distant memories gradually stopped rising from the confines of my subconscious as a new phase of my life established itself. This new phase was all about deliberate creation. I began a brand new life, in a brand new home, with a brand new set of belief systems.

Though I did not have a cent to spare, the first thing I set for myself was to turn my new home into something worthy of showcasing in a lifestyle magazine. I still needed the physical proof (for myself) that wealth was an inner state of being and was independent of money.

As it turned out, the local school had started evening classes for adults for a variety of skills. The cost was a measly $77 for an 8 week course once a week for 2 hours. I picked the one for painted finishes and one for decoupage though I didn't have a clue what that was.

We were asked to buy some pieces from the craft shop in 'papier mache' to work on. These were exorbitantly priced and were made out of flimsy crumbled paper in pathetic shapes that offended my artistic sensibilities.

I had to look elsewhere for inspiration. For the first time in my life, I actually noticed the piles of junk heaped on the curb-side of streets as garbage on council collection day. Some pieces stood out to my eyes as 'objects d'art' just needing some tender loving care. Without hesitation, I jumped out and piled the junk into my car.

I went home and spread the lot on the floor. I sat cross-legged staring at each piece and each piece stared back at me with glowing pride saying, "you and I can now bring out the inherent beauty that others are unable

45

to see." The total incongruity between my grandiose attitude and the pile of rubbish in front of me struck me as hilarious, and I rolled on the floor and laughed and laughed until sweet tears were drenching my face.

Laughing at myself was now a daily therapeutic session I indulged in with gusto.

As I was intensely intent on achieving my vision, I very quickly picked up the essence of what we were being taught. The courses were basic and geared to amateurs, and the teacher was sticking to old tried and proven methods. These were tedious to me so very quickly I adopted short-cuts that seemed to produce spectacular results.

I started visiting galleries and the most expensive furniture and art & craft shows. I no longer passed by casually admiring the exhibits but stood in front of each piece I wanted to emulate with the intention of getting into the soul of that piece. There was no analysis involved as I did not have the knowledge or skills to do so. I let it all sink in bypassing any mental processes.

I went home and went through the junk I had accumulated pulling some of the furniture apart and using various pieces for different purposes. I managed to glue some large boards together and used them as my canvas for some prints of masterpieces I had picked up at a garage sale (another haven I had discovered to stimulate the creative juices), of Botticelli, Bouguereau, and Raphael, to name a few, and used the decoupage techniques to glue them onto the boards and varnish them. They turned into exquisite pieces that left the teacher aghast: "This is not decoupage!" she cried out. "Decoupage is about piecing together various small pictures. This is incredible," she added. "What made you think of doing this? Can you show me how you did it?"

I had simply emulated some pieces I had seen selling for $2,000.00 to $4,000.00, adding my own slant from the painted finishes I was learning. If I had not done the uninspiring decoupage course, I would have never been able to work out a way to achieve such results. I applied the same technique to table tops and larger furniture pieces.

My prowess with the painted finishes was also advancing in leaps in bounds. I integrated the various finishes in the most unorthodox ways, adding copious amounts of gold paint I had bought for $2 a can to add a lavish look to the most homely of pieces.

Before I knew it, my walls were decorated with the most eye-catching adornments. In the previous house, I had practically no walls as the place was surrounded by large windows and glass doors to bring in the view. Here my walls were bare, inviting the artist within to claim its rightful place in my life.

Next, my friends asked to buy some pieces. Then I placed some ads in the paper and sold pieces I no longer had place to accommodate. The artist in me was taking over my life, and I did not suspect for one moment that one day I would be building a business around my newly found talents to sustain me for years to come but not before the right set of events had unfolded into my life to encompass the whole picture of happiness.

The first set of junk that promised me so much beauty, laughter, and joy kept to its promise and, as every day I lost myself in transforming the old dross into gold, I became aware of the alchemical processes that had been taking place beneath the surface of my mundane existence. The alchemist was coming into being.

... Daily, I contemplated these processes as they came into my conscious awareness.

~~~~~

EPISODE 2

Next, I became obsessed with my purpose in life and began sharing it with anyone who would listen. One day, as I was going on and on about this subject on the phone to a dear and very patient friend of mine, my son barged into my room. This was something he never did.

"Mother," he interrupted, "let me put you out of your misery. Your only purpose in life is to embarrass me." To which I retorted unapologetically, "If I am that bad, why did you pick me as your mother?" I had previously tried to instil in him the concept that we choose our parents before we undertake another trip to planet earth.

"It was false advertising," was the precocious response befitting the future lawyer in him.

I simply cracked up. How could I not worship this kid? He was the perfect son for me to keep me well grounded.

I was now at the outset of a new stage in my life, and I was ecstatic with where I was. Outwardly, I had taken several steps backwards in all directions but inwardly, I had acquired a new sense of freedom I had never before experienced.

Financially, I would have to rate myself as **broke** because I barely had enough money to pay the bills and no visible means of sustainable income. Inwardly, I felt **whole** because I seemed to have connected to an invisible means of support that had the knack to know what I needed and send me somehow and often the exact amount of money I required or the very thing I wanted, cost-free, in the most convoluted ways that regularly sent me into fits of laughter that rattled out of me any sense of negativity that could have infiltrated my being. Whoever was looking after me had a great sense of humour, and I loved Him for it.

The difference between my past financial state and my current state was this:

Previously, I had all the trappings of an affluent life. This entailed hard work and a lot of 'have to do's' to keep up with the lifestyle to which we had become accustomed. Keeping up with the Joneses is a never ending process which keeps you in the spiral of 'living above your means.' All it takes is a few set-backs to send you down the gurgler and into financial ruin. The fear of this happening relentlessly keeps brewing at the back of your mind and plays havoc with your emotions which are on constant alert to explode at the slightest provocation. Worry is the constant background of your life.

Currently, the futility of worrying had made itself abundantly clear as "what will be, will be." Belief in the status quo had been replaced by blind faith in the unknown and a trust that "all is well in my world, no matter what."

This was a leap in consciousness that had operated beneath the surface of my awareness and without any logical reasoning.

If logic, reason, reasoning, and hard work had let me down, I was totally open to a new state of being and "que sera sera." I was not going to question the validity of my new sense of being as it fulfilled all my needs *effortlessly* and *without worry.*

The sense of inner peace and freedom that this state of being provided me with, I would not change for all the gold in the Universe. Was this the way to find the nugget within – the Philosopher's Stone?

Call it what you will. This was a state of bliss beyond happiness as it was not attached to another human, a thing, an outcome, or ownership. This was a state where no loss was possible because of this detachment from all and despite the outward circumstances of my life. You cannot lose something you don't own, even if these are merely your own thoughts and emotions. These had subsided providing an opening for new possibilities.

Freedom
Peace
Love

These were all at my fingertips and spreading throughout my body. Sensations of delight would permeate me as I thought of these words and entered their substance and was identified by them.

Every night I submerged myself into these substances, and the darkness in my dreams had lifted and been transformed into brilliant light, a kaleidoscope of colours, and an endless stream of possibilities.

I remembered with a shudder the tone of my dreams following the collapse of my marriage and my world as I knew it then. These were recurring themes in my dreams, and they were in black and white, a precise depiction of the state of my mind and my emotions at the time.

I would dream I desperately needed to go for a swim, the water would be blue and crystal clear to start off with, but as I dove into the ocean, the whole ocean would shrink and turn into mud, drag me down, and swallow me up. I didn't know at the time that water represents the emotions, and the ocean represents the magnitude of these emotions.

In another set of dreams, I would be driving my car. It would be raining heavily, and my windscreen wiper would be broken. I couldn't see where I was going. I could not stop the car, and I knew I was heading for a collision. I have since learned that a car represents my direction in life, and rain was the internal tears I was shedding that were blocking the clarity of my vision. I obviously had no direction in life at the time, and my overwhelming emotions were drowning any sense of clarity of thought to stop the looming collision ahead.

Another telling set of dreams, and these were perhaps the most disconcerting for me, was also in black and white. I would dream I was set to sit for a test. Circumstances outside my control would prevent me from getting there on time and I would fail the test. The 'Masters' would be waiting, but I could not get there. At the time, my life seemed totally out of my control, and outside circumstances seemed to dictate my fate.

Perhaps the most telling of all of my dreams and a one-off at that: I was driving in the desert heading for an unknown destination. I was carrying 3 passengers in the back. My car had stopped, and I could not go any further. Another car was coming from the opposite direction, and the driver stopped the car, and his passenger got out and came over to ask me if I needed any help. This man was WINSTON CHURCHILL. "My car has no power," I said. "Your car has all the power you need," he replied. "Your problem is you are just following the directions of your passengers in the backseat."

'*Winston Churchill, wow!!!*' I thought upon waking. I was impressed, though I had not been impressed in my dream as 'the norm' has different connotations in the dream-state. I was puzzled though because I had no memory of ever taking any particular interest in Winston Churchill as far as historical figures are concerned.

At this point in my dreaming life, I had already been taking notice of my dreams for some time and was heavily involved in interpreting them and heeding their messages.

I figured I must have needed the advice of an influential leader in my life to pinpoint my problem and wake me up to the solution but one that I had no preconceived judgements about because I would be dragged into the analysis of his personality instead of focusing on his message.

The message was loud and clear. I was following the directions of others instead of following my own and, thus, losing my power by handing it over to them.

I resolved then and there to stop listening to others, even to my loved ones, and follow my own inner guidance. This was at the time I came to realise that so-called-well-wishers parading as my friends were feeding me lies through my brother and anonymous phone calls, and I made the decision to erect a mental wall between them and me, with spectacular consequences. (Refer to Recall 18)

Now that I had developed this connection with my dreams, I was fascinated and hell-bent on discovering every aspect of it without leaving a stone unturned.

*... **The road to Heaven was apparently through Hell, but I had discovered a portal.***

~~~~~

51

EPISODE 3

A portal is a gateway, and dreams are the mechanism that open up the gateway not only to hell and heaven, but to dimensions of reality accessible only to the initiated few. There are many reasons for this as well as many pathways.

My personal journey of discovery started with my introduction to spirituality by Oprah Winfrey, and the collection of books that fell on top of my head to wake me up from my torpor and into an alternate reality brimming with new possibilities.

My memories don't seem to be filed in a sequential order but more in terms of relevancy. The inconsequential ones get aborted. As I was typing this sentence I was struck by the dichotomy in my memory bank. The word 'sequential' is incorporated in 'inconsequential,' yet is treated as opposite in value. While relating this to you, I simultaneously have another page open where I record words that I use as 'Tools for Divination' that I am putting together as a game I wish to play with you to open you up to your psyche but for which neither you nor I are ready yet, and....

... but I digress.

The earliest recollection I have of entering this path was the realisation that meditation was the integral foundation on which all else rested. But try as I may, I could not get myself to relax. Reading that the Buddha had taught dozens of ways to meditate did not make it any easier, but I thought to myself, "Surely, there must be room for one more; who's counting?" and sought my own way.

Though I cannot swim, I find lying on my back and floating in a swimming pool the most deliciously relaxing 'non-active' activity I can engage in. It disengages me from the world outside and transports me to a world of no-constraints.

If you analyse this state of being, you will note that the juxtaposition of the words 'non-activity' with activity (and I can assure you my choice of words were truly unconscious) will, in time, bring you to the realisation that 'a world of no-constraints' is freedom itself, and that freedom comes when we are totally comfortable within any contradictions, as this liberates you from your attachment to either extreme of a point of view.

In my case, the fact that I cannot swim and yet I find floating in a pool the most relaxing state of being goes a long way to establishing that the anxiety imposed by my lack of ability to swim has no hold over me: relaxation and anxiety, 2 extremes juxtaposed ... AND THAT'S FREEDOM *as Trust becomes implicit.*

I decided to imagine myself floating in a pool every time I wanted to relax and meditate. It worked like a charm.

Without any further attempt to use my active imagination, I would find myself transported to this glorious little oasis of mine complete with lush tropical vegetation, flowers of all colours the likes of which I had only seen in altered states of consciousness, birds chirping away with happiness, and a crystal clear pond inviting me to dive in with open arms. I would then be transformed into a nymph that turned into a mermaid as I plunged into the soothing, refreshing, and ultimately cleansing water in my psyche. I would lose myself in this scenery where I could swim like a fish, only to re-emerge in my terrestrial life as though reborn anew. These experiences felt just as real as my daily waking life, only the sensations were much more intense.

This was a regular escape route for me, from which I did not wish to return and I thought would always be available to me. Unfortunately (?), this was just a preliminary initiation into other realities which I was being groomed for, that I had no inkling of at the time.

The first deviation from this regular scenario was the day when in the midst of my swimming session as a mermaid, I suddenly remembered I could not swim. Frantically, I struggled to swim ashore and, seized by panic, I began to drown. A dolphin appeared out of nowhere, glided under me, and lifted me up to breath air into my 'human' lungs that were gasping for air.

This was the first time my conscious awareness had intruded into my subconscious realm and the two had come face-to-face. The barriers between the 2 worlds were cracking and a portal had opened up. I, of course, was thoroughly unaware of what was going on inside of me and what was in store for me.

I have to clarify that these sessions were not dreams or visions, nor were they visualisations or imagination in its normal accepted context. I was awake at the time, but in an altered state of consciousness, without any control over what was to unfold. I was inside the scene with all my 5 senses experiencing it. *I was simply being.* I wouldn't know how else to describe it.

Dreams are an internal process with no objective reality, and we operate from inside the dream without any rhyme or reason or conscious control. They happen **in the sleep state.** We're inside the dream and have no control over it, but all our senses are alive and heightened in the experience of the dream. Our analytical processes are suspended.

Visions are also outside of our control but happen as an objective reality projected outside of ourselves that we bear witness to **in a semi-waking altered state of consciousness.** The vision is outside of us, and we have no control over it nor do we comprehend it at the time. Our analytical faculties are also suspended.

Visualisation is an objective, active process totally within our control, experienced **in the waking state.** We exercise the power of choice and take control of the images that we wilfully project outside of us.

Imagination is an active/passive process where we are in control of the choices we make as far as the subject of our imagination is concerned but often have no control over what these will bring back to us or where they will take us. Observation is internal **in the alpha waking state.**

... I was opening up to the various modalities of the states of consciousness.

~~~~

EPISODE 4

After the initial deviation from my habitual sessions in the cleansing waters of my psyche, I must have been ready for the next stage in my progression. Apparently, it was time for me to change my modus operandi as far as meditation was concerned. I don't know if this was a conscious choice or a subconscious drive but to give my relaxation a kick-start I now changed from Imagining myself floating in a swimming pool to floating on a fluffy, heavenly, soft hunk of cloud and let myself go to where the fancy took me, with no expectation whatsoever or any preconceived idea.

This new model seemed just as satisfactory for relaxation purposes, but the experience that followed was entirely different and just as bewildering.

I was aware of my inert body on the bed, but my senses were transported up with the 2nd **'ME'** floating about a metre above the body on this heavenly cloud. Up there, there was no room for worldly problems or anxiety; utter peace and bliss were the state of my being. It was a totally sensual experience...

... until a **'3rd ME'** popped up above the **'ME'** on the cloud, looked down on the **'2nd ME'** and exclaimed **"I'M ANDROGYNOUS!"**. This **'3rd ME'** was **ME** at 4½ years old, and the body she was looking down on with bewilderment was just a ghostly outline of a figure, a mere effigy of myself, like the chalk figures the police draw around dead people to indicate where the body was lying at the time of death in an accident or murder scene.

"How could she tell '*"I/ME/WE/US is androgynous by looking at an outline of a figure?"*' I began to wonder when I was interrupted. On my right-hand side, a fat woman in her forties, prematurely grey (who didn't look anything like the **ME** I am accustomed to), was admonishing the child: "If you didn't know we are androgynous, who is supposed to know?" She was an insufferable 'nag' and I wanted to banish her from life (the **'4th ME'** – the critic - oh yuk!)

To complete the picture, I was now encapsulated, on my left-hand side, into Rodin's statue "The Thinker" in all his glorious nakedness pondering: '*"What am I supposed to make of all this?"*' (You guessed it – this was the **'5th ME'** – the analytical self), *masculine, I might add.*

Indeed...

... *But which 'ME' am "I"?*

I had just been formally introduced to the various personalities that run my life:

- A corpse (brought to life to experience terrestrial reality through the 5 senses)
- A ghost (the essence of the soul)
- A child (who had established the rules for my life at the age of 4½)
- A nag (or the inner critic, that I have since sent on long service leave with a one-way ticket)
- A thinker (in charge of the choice-making mechanism which sets the direction in life)

This much I understood, and I was not impressed.

But what I did not suspect was the deep transformation that was taking place inside of me.

Remember I mentioned in one of my earliest episodes that at the age of 4½ I had decided I did not want to be a girl, changed my name to a boy's name, and only wanted to respond to that name? This inner urge to identify with male characteristics lasted until I turned 12 and nature imposed its own agenda on me, and I reluctantly relinquished my innermost desire.

Well, it wasn't until years later that all became crystal clear to me when I came across this passage from **the Gospel of Thomas** (and I am not a bible reader):

Simon Peter said to them:

"Let Mary go out from among us,
Because women are not worthy of the life."

Jesus said:

"See, I shall lead her
So that I will make her male,
That she too may become a living spirit
Resembling you males.
For every woman who makes herself male
Will enter the kingdom."

Also from the Gospel of Thomas

"When you make the Two One,
and when you make the Inside like the Outside
and the Outside like the Inside,
and the Above like the Below,
and when you make the Male and the Female One and the Same,
then you will enter the Kingdom of God".

What strange words and avant-garde concepts.

But these are exactly the teachings on the Emerald Tablet of the Hermetic Tradition that Alchemists have been trying to decipher for millennia to discover the secret to eternal life and eternal youth.

This man called 'Jesus' was an absolute genius. He understood the laws of creation like no-one could. He was the original Alchemist from way, way back, and he was lethal. The world was not ready for him; he had to be exterminated.

His followers and any followers of these doctrines were also tortured and put to death systematically and mercilessly so eventually they had to go underground and the knowledge was sealed into secrecy.

For the time being, it was sufficient for me to realise that my 4½ year old had finally reconciled her Male and Female counterparts and was ready for some 'alchemistry.'

... We were ready to explore the Above and the Below.

~~~~~

EPISODE 5

Below is the Natural world. Above is the Super-Natural.

The Super-Natural, as the name implies, is the superior form of the natural, as I had come to understand it.

I also understood that the Natural Self belonged to the Individual Self and that the Super-Natural Self belonged to the Divine Self.

Scientists were now asserting that, in the Holographic Universe, the Microcosm reflects the Macrocosm, which, in essence, is saying what the hermetic tradition has been saying all along that the Individual Self reflects the Divine Self.

Basically we have 2 selves:

the Individual Self which is the smaller self that is limited to earthly personal experiences and interpretations attached to them

and

the Divine Self which is the expanded self of who we are that holds all the potentialities allocated to humankind.

Through my readings I had come across the terms: the Lower Self and the Higher Self to refer to these 2 states of being, and I found these to be adequate for me to explore these selves.

Through the weird phenomena that I had been experiencing spasmodically, I had glimpsed some of the possibilities available to the Higher Self. Naturally, I wanted to access more and more of these...

... But how?

Though I enjoyed them thoroughly, at the very real risk of being treated as a lunatic, these were spontaneous and out of my control, and I wanted to be in the driver's seat.

My natural life was following the bell curve generated by the ups and downs of daily events. I found out that the less I focused on them, the less they affected me internally, and the less input they needed from me to adjust themselves. All I had to do was to attend to my daily needs and the task at hand; the rest took care of itself.

I diverted all my energies to the graph that charted my ascension to the Higher realms. I envisioned a missile that would take me straight to the top and land me in heaven.

A straight line, it was not. My missile preferred to take me via the slow scenic route, hitting many dead-ends and cul-de-sacs, and some very enchanting territory.

Reading was making me eager to acquire these powers, and I was amply soothed and rewarded internally and externally, but these rewards were erratic and mercurial. I wanted more consistent results.

I figured that if I truly wanted to take charge of my evolution I had to start putting into action some of the things I learnt ...

... But where does one start?

If I am to opt out of the linear concept of life, I thought to myself, then any point is a good point, as it will lead me back to the beginning: the A, B, C of creation.

So I started with the most ludicrous, in search of a sign.

One of the books that patiently sat on my girlfriend's shelf, gathering dust and waiting for the right moment for me to arrive, was Linda Goodman's *Star Signs* that fell on my head to wake me up to a new reality.

This was an altogether fascinating book, but the chapter that got me enthralled was the one on Lexigrams, the ancient codes that reveal the hidden meaning of words.

Everyone is familiar with anagrams, a word game played for intellectual exercise and amusement. Lexigrams are a play on anagrams, except that Linda adds mystery to the game by trying to explore the hidden meaning within words.

Could words really penetrate the mysteries of the Universe? Could they reveal the hidden secrets of creation? Could they be used as a tool for divination?

Let's start with the word **"divination"**: divin-ation.

The dictionary defines **divination** as the practice of seeking knowledge of the future or the unknown by supernatural means.

The dictionary defines **divine** as "of, from, or like God."

ation or **tion** tacked to the end of a word denotes **action.**

So...

divination can be construed to mean **Godlike action** that leads to divine knowledge, the future, and the unknown.

Is it a coincidence that the word divination includes the divine or what is of God?

*Could I possibly access my **Divine Self** through a **tool for divination?***

Was this the right tool?

This leads to staggering possibilities when you consider the notion in the Bible:

... In the Beginning was the Word.

~~~~

EPISODE 6

I have used my own version of Lexigrams to gain insights from words, and I will share these with you as I go along.

The first one that hit me between the eyes was the word **Intellect.**

I had just signed up for a course in hypnosis, and I was fascinated by the childish simplicity of the wording used to induce hypnosis:

I want you to take 3 deep breaths and relax,
Now I want you to breathe deeply and evenly,
Deeply and evenly and relax.
Now I want you to concentrate,
close your eyes and concentrate.
I want you to imagine that there is a blackboard in front of you,
and on the blackboard are written the words Deep Sleep.
Concentrate on these words,
see these words,
and gradually you will feel yourself becoming sleepier and sleepier ...

The latter part of this mantra would be repeated several times until the subject fell into a trance.

It was repeated further if a deeper trance-state was needed.

And it worked, though sleep hardly describes the state you're in, as you are able to hear and respond to the hypnotist, and your senses and ability to remember are heightened, as well as your susceptibility to suggestions, while your critical faculties are suspended.

How could such simple words take you from the control-freaks that we all are, to a state where you gratefully surrender complete control of your mind to a virtual stranger?

What was even more fascinating was that this stranger could take you to places in your mind where you yourself had lost sight of. Subterranean memories no longer available to you, he could unearth with the simple suggestion: "I want you to go back to a time in your life when..."

Was this a suggestion, was this a command, or was this a direction? ... hmm!!!

To add further depth to the fascination, what unfolded next was not a simple exercise in recovering a lost memory, but you actually went back in time (as a time traveller would) and relived the experience as though the rest of your life had not mattered, and you were actually back there trapped into that memory with all its visual, its sensual, & its emotional context intact, dictating the rules of the rest of your life.

Further ...

... the reliving of this memory, with all the trauma entailed, relieved you of the anguish associated with it, and which you had not been aware of; yet, you had not been able to release it because your awareness of it had been dimmed and you were no longer in possession of that circumstance and, therefore, it was outside of your control in 'the **NOW** moment.'

It struck me that the words **now** and **own** are anagrams. *Was this a coincidence?*

Let's analyse the play of these words and where they lead us.

You must **own** the circumstance in the **now,** in other words claim **owner*ship*** (the **ship** of the **owner** that takes him to his destination), for you to be able to give it up. Simply put: you cannot give up what you don't own. We inadvertently keep ownership of that which we deny, even if it is something that is destroying us.

The secret to **release** (re-lease, a new lease) is in first claiming something as our own so we can place ourselves in a position to give it up.

The formula: Own + give up = release

How ingenious!

In this convoluted Universe, the metaphor in these simple words had the capacity to take me directly to the crux of the matter. I had moved from baffled to **"I KNOW."**

Curious: how **now** & **own** are part of the word k**now.**

I think it would be wise of me to quit right here before I drive you insane. You have no idea how much restraint I had to exercise so I didn't dissect several other words in my dialogue above that I could use to demonstrate how you can use words as a tool for divination in order to access their hidden message, which are hardly hidden when we look at them with certain eyes.

But you get my drift.

I will spare you for now, but I want you to guess:

*... **What hidden message has the word INTELLECT for us?***

~~~~~

EPISODE 7

INTELLECT = in-tell-elect

And that's precisely the function of the intellect. It's what you elect to tell yourself.

Hallelujah, what a discovery !!!

It didn't take long for me to marry the powers vested in words, the faculties of the intellect and the secrets of the hypnotic mind, to carve myself a fool-proof system for self-hypnosis.

Hypnosis is largely based on the power of suggestion (what you accept as the truth that others dish out to you but ***more importantly,*** what you elect to tell yourself.)

I had already learned that all you need for hypnosis is:

A relaxed attitude (You don't have to go into trance for that; you can be in a continuous relaxed state once you learn how to give up fear and doubt and replace it with trust – more easily said than done but still mandatory)

Relinquishing control to the therapist (in this case, my 'other self' would have to serve as the therapist)

Trust (my invisible helpers had already gained my trust in the Universe)

Excited, I grabbed myself a piece of paper and scribbled in large letters:

I am now going to have
FUN
FUN
FUN
!!!

I rang Mariana, the organiser of a Singles Group that a friend had recommended. I introduced myself, but having second thoughts that sent shivers down my back, I cut the conversation short and promised to ring her when I was ready.

I then picked up the phone and rang my friend Tanya who had been trying for months to get me out of the house seeking fun "for a change."

I said, "Tanya, tomorrow we're going to the Mosman Rowers Club. They have Jazz on; I love Jazz. We are going to sit outside, enjoying glorious weather and a mouth-watering steak. We are then going to be surrounded by these gorgeous single men all fighting over us ..."

She interrupted. "My, my, you've changed your tune, what's happened? But I've got news for you: you can only get in if you are a member or get signed-in by a member. Also, you need a booking. This place is booked out 2 weeks ahead."

I chided, "Don't be so negative; we're going."

She was right. The restaurant was booked out and what made matters worse was that half the restaurant was screened off because some party had booked the venue for a private function.

Before Tanya could say "I told you so," I spotted a big round table on the deck beyond the restaurant and some glass doors. I asked the receptionist if that was part of the restaurant, to which she replied "No." "Could we please, please sit out there? We promise we won't make any noise," I pleaded against my nature.

The receptionist then asked for proof of membership. Tanya stared at me with lips clenched. I stared back with slumped shoulders. Whereupon a couple appeared. The woman was young, beautiful, and vivacious. She took one look at me and asked "Are you Ani by any chance?" I had never met the woman. "How do you know?" I asked puzzled. "I am psychic" she replied playfully, "My name is Marianna."

She signed us in and when she heard we were sitting outside because we couldn't get a booking, she decided they would join us at our large table that could accommodate another 6.

As we engaged in conversation, the room divider that was used to separate the other party was drawn back and revealed a crowd of people seemingly having fun, as their laughter drowned our conversation.

Marianna looked up and said, "Ah, there is a singles party going on there."

I said "No, I was told this was a fund-raising charity for the Cancer Foundation."

She put me wise by explaining, "I know this group of people. They are all single but the founder, Ian, is a good friend of mine who supports several charities and organises functions to raise money for these charities."

It was then that I spotted Paul, the husband of my dear friend, Susan, talking to Ian. I decided to take it upon myself to get Paul to explain his presence at a singles party.

I made my way across to the other party, said hello to Paul, who introduced me to Ian, just as someone tapped on my shoulder and I turned around to be embraced by Susan.

Susan proceeded to explain that Paul's brother was single, he had 2 tickets to the charity, he couldn't make it, so gave the tickets to Susan.

Before long we were back at our table with Susan, her husband, and 4 eligible bachelors passing their business cards around and exchanging phone numbers.

The scene unfolded just as I had predicted, and I could not stop laughing all night.

The next day, Ian rang me and asked me out.

... And for 9 months I had FUN, FUN, FUN!!!

~~~~~

EPISODE 8

Ian was like a child. He had forgotten to grow up. He had a little red sports car that he delighted in driving at full speed over speed humps so the car would take off like a flying saucer and land with a thud. He thought he was at Luna Park.

The thud, followed by uncontrollable bursts of laughter, dissolved any residue of knots lodged in my solar plexus.

Another one of his pleasures was chasing me on the beach at 2:00 a.m. in his tuxedo and bare feet, after a formal dinner or party which he was fond of attending, where he was regularly invited because of his charming personality.

Ian delighted the 4½-year-old in me and our relationship remained at that level which, at that stage of my life, was just perfect for me.

One night I got home at 2:00 a.m. and, excited with happiness, I could not get to sleep. I thought of an activity that would keep my mind occupied without making any noise so I wouldn't wake up my son.

I remembered a book a friend, who lived interstate and was on a short visit to my home town, had given me with the following warning, "I came across this book and felt compelled to buy it. I know it's meant for you, but I want you to promise me that you will never talk to me about it." The book was about Psychic Development, but I can't remember the exact title.

The book outlined certain breathing exercises that promised to produce various degrees of altered states of consciousness, each designed for a particular end in mind. One set of exercises was about Astral Travel but when I read that there was a possibility of encountering malevolent entities, I decided to avoid that particular exercise. It did, however, add that it was simple to control these entities the same way as you would control your emotions.

I was aware enough to realise that at that point in my life I had very little control over my emotions; therefore, my chances of subduing evil entities were not something I wanted to contemplate.

I settled for an exercise that took you through the process of relaxing your body and mind and charging up your energy through a particular series of breathing exercises, then visualising a small point of light and watching it grow bigger.

All throughout our house we had dimmers, and at night time I dimmed several of the lights so we could find our way to the bathroom or other rooms without bumping into doors and furniture.

The light above my bed was also dimmed when I started the exercises, and I got to the point where I could actually see this small speck of light at the right hand corner of my eye, near the ceiling.

To my bewilderment, the light got bigger and bigger, spinning vigorously, and started moving towards the light globe in the ceiling. By the time it had joined up with the globe, I had covered my eyes panic stricken, while trying to suppress cries of terror. Simultaneously I heard several, successive bangs and all the lights in the house went out.

My son, awaken by the noise, came rushing to my room banging into doors. "What's happening? What have you done?" He yelled. "I don't know, I think we have a power overload," I explained weakly. "What power overload at this hour with a few dimmer lights?" was his obvious response.

I asked him to go to bed, and we would investigate in the morning. In the morning, we checked the power board and the power overload switch was flicked off. Perhaps he didn't want to question me any further as that would be risking admission that the possibility of tampering with such power was within my grasp.

Needless to say, I suspended further experimentation. Unfortunately, I subsequently lent the book to someone who appeared and disappeared out of my life mysteriously and this knowledge was lost on me for good.

... Why was this power introduced into my life, then taken away?

~~~~~

EPISODE 9

One day, Ian rang me and said with some reservation, "This is embarrassing, my company is having a formal dinner to give out prizes for performance and accomplishment. I am awarded first prize, but they are having name tags printed for the guests and after all this time I don't even know what your surname is."

"My surname is Preston" I offered.

"Preston, Preston," he repeated. "You are not by any chance related to Levy Preston?" he asked hesitantly.

"Intimately" I responded.

On the way to the celebratory dinner, he drove at the speed limit. Most of the night, he was very quiet though he held me tight as we danced and told me I looked ravishing.

That night he drove me straight home and confessed that he found the idea of continuing to see me disturbing as Levy Preston was a business associate of his and had become a good friend. In fact, the night before he was at his place negotiating a training session with his company, and the thought of him dating a friend's wife went against his principles.

Begging and pleading my case are not some of my strong points and letting go to make room for something better had become second nature to me, so exercising empathy, I looked at the situation from his point of view and agreed to part but stay friends.

"But," I added. "What do we do with the tickets we have for next Saturday's cocktail party?"

"There is no reason we can't go as friends," he suggested. And we have remained friends to this day.

At the cocktail party, I moved around talking to various people I knew. But every time I moved, I noticed a pair of big, brown, beautiful eyes hovering over all the heads and resting on me, making me blush to the core, though blushing is not something suited to my complexion. This pair of eyes belonged to a hunk of man rarely encountered in real life.

This man was accompanied by a woman.

I decided to leave to alleviate my discomfort. As I reached the door forcing my way through the crowds, the couple had also moved closer to the exit. I had to pass them on my way out and brushed against the woman, who grabbed me by the arm and alarmingly declared: "This man has been watching you all night. He can't take his eyes off you. My name is Lucinda, this is Justin, what is yours?

She then proceeded to ask me a whole lot of personal questions which revealed that Justin was involved in the same business I had once been involved in, and I was contemplating its revival. Justin gave me his card just in case I wanted to get back into that field.

For one week, I did not sleep. The image of him haunted me day and night. The fact that I did not have a business to speak of was a huge deterrent to use as an excuse to ring him. The fact that he was much, much younger than me was another, but my biggest hang-up was that he was with another woman.

"But she was the one introducing us and he gave me his card in front of her," I advised myself.

Daily, my friends encouraged me to ring him. "What have you got to lose?" they asked.

My head, my heart, and my self-respect were a few things I could think of, but it would be well worth it just for one night, so it was that I relented. I rang. After a very brief, awkward conversation he suggested to come over and discuss the possibilities open to us.

I had forgotten how exquisitely beautiful he looked. When I opened the door and looked into his eyes, my heart dropped, my jaw dropped, and he blushed to the core.

*... **What were the Gods thinking?***

~~~~~

EPISODE 10

I have no recollection of how we ended up in bed but every cell in my body still remembers the thrill of his touch and the feel of his sensuous muscular body, designed perfectly to bring supreme ecstasy to any woman's senses.

This must be what the angels abdicated heaven for and fell to earth.

That night I didn't sleep a wink so I wouldn't miss a second of the euphoria his presence created even when he was in deep sleep. I kept wishing in the deepest recesses of my heart that this could last for the rest of the week. As luck would have it, my husband and my son were away interstate for the week.

The next morning, as I was preparing breakfast, my friend Renee walked through the French doors that I often forgot to lock, just as Justin came in from the bathroom after having a shower, with a skimpy towel wrapped around his loins.

The look Renee gave him caused him to almost drop the towel he was hanging on to, so he made a quick dash back to the bedroom, blushing as he customarily did whenever a woman gave him that usual lustful look; which was often.

Renee couldn't control her awe "Is this a real man or is it Adonis himself that you snatched from the Heavens with your magic?"

Over breakfast, I discovered that, coincidentally, the night we met he, too, was breaking up with the woman he was with, his girlfriend, and that they had agreed to remain friends.

Justin and I liked the same exotic foods, the same Latin American Music, the same quality of art, and my newly acquired attitude of "let it be" matched perfectly his long held belief of living in the moment, non-judgement, no expectations or demands placed on another, a love of nature and animals, and a boundless tolerance for individual idiosyncrasies.

This man had such a heart of gold that made his extraordinary good looks fade into insignificance.

To have simply known that such a man exists restored your faith in life. To have spent one night with him was a gift from the Gods, but for that night to stretch into a week, and then weeks, months and years, was plainly beyond my own realm of imagination or expectation. The man was bliss personified.

Justin's only problem in life was his dissatisfaction with his career as he did not have a clear vision of how he wanted it to unfold. This also reflected my own dilemma at the time as I urgently needed large amounts of money to get me out of the financial hole I was in.

Nonetheless, we fell into each other's life easily and effortlessly without any plan or consideration for the future.

... The Gods forged their own plan for us.

~~~~~

EPISODE 11

My relationship with Ian had been different. It was a platonic one and I kept him away from my son and my home, so my husband never knew about it, but the minute he found out about my new relationship with Justin he moved back in with his luggage and his baggage.

I could hardly object; he owned half the house. So long as he stayed in a separate bedroom I could manage the inconvenience.

Immediately, though, he began badgering me about the unsuitability of my relationship and its presage of doom and gloom as well as the negative effects it would have on our son, totally oblivious to his own relationship with another woman and its life-altering consequences.

Normally, I would have fought back defending myself and pointing out his own indiscretions. With my newly integrated system of belief, I took 3 deep breaths to calm me down and allow me to tap into my new sense of being, and I heard myself saying "Levy, this is my life and my personal problems, allow me to deal with them myself. You just focus on your own life."

With that said, I walked away calmly as I knew innately that I had permanently shut the door to that line of conversation. I was amazed at how easy, smooth, and soothing this new experience had been.

Allowing him his life as he chose it without judgement and allowing myself the same privilege had introduced a much needed balance in the area of relationships.

On the weekend, I briefly introduced my son to Justin as he came to pick me up for a surprise outing. I didn't know where he was taking me, so I dressed up to the hilt. It turned out he had planned a romantic picnic on the beach with seafood and French champagne.

All was perfect except that whimsical nature decided to blow a gale which sent handfuls of golden smooth sand up my skirt, my nose, and every cavity in my body. My beautiful, silken, glossy hair was turned into a matted mop and traces of red lipstick all over my face hinted at a passionate encounter. Fortunately for me, there were no mirrors on the beach.

When we arrived home and my son greeted Justin with "What did you do to my mother? She was in mint condition when you picked her up," I knew the two would hit it off and become friends.

As I fell into Justin's gentle ways by osmosis, I introduced him to my magical ways which he found hard to believe but which he regarded with intrigue and much amusement. He would shake his head and say, "You're crazy" and roll his head back with laughter.

I took advantage of his leniency and integrated him into my crazy ways anyway.

The first one on anyone's books is of course parking spots. You visualise a parking spot and, voila, it's there waiting for you when you get there. Visualisation is not my forte, so I use the power of intent, using words to direct an outcome like, "When we get there, there will be someone leaving and vacating the spot for us."

This can happen with monotonous regularity but will still be put down to coincidence, so I upgraded it to a more deliberate approach like: getting there, selecting a particular spot, positioning the car to drive into that spot, putting the indicator on, reclining my seat to indicate a relaxed posture of expectancy, "I am in no hurry, I know the driver of this car will come any minute now and move out so I can take his spot, no need to rush or panic." 90% of the time the driver materialised within one minute.

I was learning and teaching.

... The truth/reality "lies" within the contractions !!!

~~~~~

EPISODE 12

Contradictions abounded in my life.

My marriage broke up and my life turned upside down in the most idyllic of settings. My home, the bush that surrounded it, the tranquil water views, the birds and the bees all promised heaven on earth. My inner life had been undergoing hell.

I had now lost that material promise, my marital circumstances had not changed to the better, my financial situation sucked, yet inwardly I felt I was in heaven and I valued every scrap of happiness the Universe threw my way. I started each day with a long list of things I was grateful for. I soon found out there were many.

I ardently pursued this new line of knowledge and hungrily devoured every morsel of information I could get hold of. And at every opportunity, I put it into practice without challenging its validity.

My husband had extended his business interstate where he had moved his girlfriend to give himself a legitimate excuse to stay with her with impunity. I don't know why he persisted in the charade, but I wasn't going to question it as it suited me fine.

He normally stayed away for 2 weeks at a time, and I looked forward to his departure so Justin could come and stay. I would stay at his place on the weekends that my husband was home, but I preferred Justin to stay because I missed my son and my place was more suitable for entertaining our mutual friends, which grew in numbers as we became the golden couple.

One Monday morning, as my husband had packed up to leave and I was looking forward to him going, he had a glitch with his computer and he could not print the manuals necessary for his business presentation. He was panicking and so was I, each for our own reasons. By the time he got everything fixed, there was very little time to get to the airport on time to catch his plane. He threw his hands up in despair.

Much to his surprise (and mine), I offered to drive him. "What good would that do? You're a lousy driver, and there isn't enough time to get there at this hour of the day" he yelled.

"For one thing, it will save you time in finding parking for your car and lumbering your suitcases from the car park to the foyer." Besides, I have a special deal with the Traffic Angel. Justin had found a little plastic, silver statue that you wound up and its wings would flap, so your Traffic

Angel would clear the way for you. I loved my traffic Angel and promptly installed her in my car.

Without further time to waste, we jumped in my car and I asked him to do the driving as he was the more competent driver, provided, of course, he followed my instructions.

"Competent in your case means aggressive. Add frustration, anxiety and impatience to the mix, and you have a recipe for failure. Now, if you want to get there on time, you need to relax and slow down," I explained.

He gave me a dirty look and hit the accelerator. We hit the first red traffic light, he hit on the breaks, and I hit the dashboard. Before the light had time to turn green, he had taken off and continued at great speed until he hit the second red traffic light.

"Now that you know for sure we have Buckley's chance of making it, you can take a deep breath, let go, relax, and slow down" I offered.

There were no right turns in sight so he slowed right down with every intention of turning back. However, the next traffic light was green. And the next. And the next. And the next.

"See what I mean" I remarked.

"Oh, that's just a coincidence. One is bound to hit green lights sometimes. Just wait until we get to Boundary Street. The bottleneck is horrendous, and it takes for ever to get through. I drive this way every couple of weeks, and I know what I am talking about" he asserted.

"Just keep at this speed" I instructed.

At the bottleneck, we sailed through; we had not hit one red traffic light till then. We didn't hit another red light until we got to the airport on time, with 5 minutes to spare. As we got his luggage out of the boot, with a big smile on my face, I wished him good luck, success, and a great time, because I was looking forward to the same for me with Justin.

"Witch," he called me and half smiled.

That was just an experiment. I was dazed.

*... **What had just happened?***

~~~~~

EPISODE 13

Another instance that comes to mind was at the end of my son's school year when prizes were given out for scholastic achievements.

Our son was Ducks of the Year and was to receive several prizes. As usual we were running late, so we decided to drop him off in front of the venue and go in search of a parking spot.

As soon as we had deposited him, my husband jumped on the accelerator and headed off towards the obscure end of town. "Where are you going so fast?" I asked. "We are going to miss all the parking spots." "There will be no parking spots at this busy end of town as you know. We have to get right out if we want to find a parking spot," he argued, having spotted a "Full" sign at the parking station.

"But I can't walk so far in my high heels" I explained, trying to bring some sense into his head. He ignored me. "You're wasting precious time. There will be no parking spots at that end," I insisted. "That's ridiculous. You know we stand a better chance there." "NO! You'll see," is all I could say in defiance.

Of course, we could not find a parking spot no matter how hard he looked, searching frantically.

"I am going home" he announced, defeated, and turned back heading for home, forgetting that our son would be devastated if we didn't attend the celebrations.

As we approached our venue, I grabbed him by the arm. "Slow down, slow down, there is a parking spot for us right here" I confided. "Where?" he asked, his eyes rotating from side to side. "I don't know, just about here," I whispered.

Exasperation was evident on his face as tension spread throughout his entire body. He once again jumped on the accelerator as this had become his automatic response to dealing with my nonsense. Just then, a pedestrian jumped in front of our car and slumped on the bonnet as my husband jumped on the breaks, with the same vigour, in a bid to avoid crushing the innocent man to death.

The pedestrian was drunk but otherwise unhurt. He collected himself and walked ahead as though nothing serious had taken place. Meanwhile, the traffic lights had turned red and we couldn't proceed. By the time they turned green again, our victim had walked towards a car past the traffic lights, climbed into the driver's seat, and drove off.

All we had to do was glide into the space he had just vacated.

"That's the spot I was telling you about," I announced with great relief and glee. We were parked directly opposite our venue.

"Witch," he called me with mixed feelings.

These kinds of occurrences were becoming a daily event in life. I shared them with my friends and encouraged them to do the same. One of my happiest moments was when a timid friend of mine came over and excitedly shared her story with me.

"You know the lounge suite I've been saving up for the last 2 years? Well, it costs $6,500, and I have managed to save only $4,500. Today I went to David Jones once again to make sure that model was still available for sale but with

a new sense of urgency. I kept thinking to myself, I can't possibly wait another year of saving for this; I want it now. How would Ani do it? I went upstairs with new resolve, not knowing quite what to expect. To my huge surprise, the lounge suite was reduced to $4,500 just for the day."

"A woman was sitting on the sofa while her husband was negotiating with the salesman, then reporting back to his wife. She wanted it at all price, but he wasn't very keen because it was too pretty and frilly for his taste."

"At one moment, while the husband had his back turned to the salesperson, I grabbed him by the arm, pulled him aside, and said: 'I want this lounge suite, I want it now, and here is my DJ credit card, or I can give you a cheque. They are still thinking about it. I have made up my mind. I have been a faithful client of DJ's for 10 years, I deserve some consideration. But if I walk out of here, I am not coming back.'"

"It's yours," he said without hesitation, as he was sick and tired of the couple's indecision."

"You know I have been practicing with the parking spots, and they have really been working for me. I thought why not use the same mindset you taught me with the lounge suite. I am simply stunned at how this works, she stated with obvious mirth, and gave me a big, warm hug."

This was a contagious way of life. Sharing these stories with my friends, setting ourselves new parameters of achievement, and revelling in our conquests became a favourite pastime of ours, as we recounted, relished, and celebrated our adventures whenever we got together.

... With so much to look forward to, looking back was a thing of the past.

~~~~~

EPISODE 14

Ordinary solutions to everyday problems were no longer satisfactory. The more EXTRA-ordinary the solution, the higher the appeal it now held for me for my Psychic Development.

I had a timber fence, around 1.8 meters, dividing my land and the neighbour's. I had a beautiful Jasmine vine growing wildly over it, but it often needed pruning. Unfortunately, the neighbours had a savage dog that went hysterical every time I approached the fence. One day, as I was fixing the Jasmine vine, the dog could not contain itself at just barking but, possessed with rage, jumped so high that it managed to nip one of my fingers and draw blood.

I paid a visit to my lovely neighbours laying out the problem. They invited me in for tea and cake and explained that the poor dog did not have the ability to understand that what it was doing was wrong. It soon became very clear that my neighbours had even less of an ability to comprehend that there was a course of action they could take to prevent carnal damage.

They also told me, within the ensuing 2 hours, that the poor dog was confined to a small garden and had no other way of vesting its frustration. However, this was a house they had inherited from their grandparents. They loved and cherished it, and they were looking forward to passing it on to their own children and grandchildren in time.

Clearly, no amount of persuasion would work with these delightful people.

I needed a miracle. "No," I corrected myself. "I need magic."

I had by now discovered that asking for a miracle was tantamount to asking for trouble, as an ominous situation was a pre-requisite to a miracle. I wasn't going to wait for this dog to go feral and find the strength to jump over the fence, or mow it down, and rip me to shreds, so I could undergo an NDE and be snatched back to life by some miracle, and henceforth be forever grateful for an extension of life, albeit with a mutilated body.

There had to be a different way. *But what?*

"ASK AND IT SHALL BE GIVEN"

And so it was that I came across a little book on magic that explained that if you wanted to get rid of negative neighbours or some such, all you have to do is get a mirror, face it in the direction of what you want to get rid of, and state your intention.

Could it be that simple?

Ah, but there was a proviso: under no circumstances should you wish any harm to come to the other, as this will eventually bounce back on you.

I had no desire to harm this dog or have it put down. I just wanted it OUT OF MY LIFE with my very best wishes.

I quickly found a mirror, stated my wish clearly and loudly so I could be heard, and promptly got side-tracked by life.

A month had lapsed, and I had completely forgotten the issue.

Our garage faced a back street, and as I used to drive everywhere, I seldom had a reason to go to the front of the house.

On this particular day, as I was driving to an appointment, I suddenly remembered I had forgotten an important document I needed to discuss at this meeting. So I made a quick U-turn and decided it would be faster to pull up in front of the house and run in to fetch the document.

As I came to a halt, I noticed a large Real Estate sign in front of my neighbour's property with "SOLD" across it. I couldn't resist the temptation, so I ran in and asked what was going on.

"You wouldn't believe it," my charming neighbour told me excitedly. "The weekend after you were here last, we went for a drive to the country and came across this huge, beautiful property, 2 acres would you believe, going for a song. We decided to buy it then and there as we thought the grand children would love it and it would be heaven for our dog to run around to its heart's content. We couldn't wait for contracts of the sale to come through and the owners agreed to look after our dog until we moved in, so we took him over a couple of days later, and he is as happy as Larry."

That would explain why I had so easily forgotten about the issue as the dog was no longer around, barking and claiming my attention.

But how do you explain my neighbour's change of heart regarding the family treasures and passing them on to the children and grandchildren?

I have used this method successfully on many occasions and taught my friends to do the same, with gratuitous results. On the one occasion when one of my friends, despite my warnings, went ahead and used the mirror to get her neighbours to move but could not find it in her heart to wish them well. She ended up selling and moving out herself, and it took her a whole year before she could settle into her new house, while she had to waste exorbitant amounts of money on rent and twice as much as she had budgeted for on her home renovations.

She confronted me later and said the mirror didn't work for her. I said it did, perfectly, as it was meant to. She couldn't wish them well so her wish bounced back on her.

So if you decide to use this method, always remember to wish the other a better outcome in lieu of what they will be losing. Wish them to move into a better environment where they will be exquisitely happy. And if that bounced back on you, surely you wouldn't complain about moving to a better place where you are exquisitely happy.

Some people are unable to grasp the importance of the second half of the equation and can do themselves untold harm. Use your head and your heart in balance.

I can understand that it is sometimes hard to wish another well while they're making your life miserable but why is it so hard to wish them well once they're out of your life and can't affect it one way or the other?

... Your happiness is never contingent on someone else's unhappiness.

~~~~~

EPISODE 15

Of course I knew that the mirror was not the thing that brought my wishes into manifestation. It was the power of intention that did it. The mirror simply serves to focus your attention and intention. It is just a crutch until you learn to use the power of the mind without props.

The problem is that without props you tend to slide back into default mode. Default mode is set at the collective expectations of your society.

Perhaps I should mention here that a major contributing factor to my predisposition to magic was the tales of wisdom that my dad used to recount as my bedtime and daytime stories. These were based on the lore of Hodja the Trickster, which to my mind equates with the Fool of the Tarot and Confucius.

Dad amused me with an endless array of magical tricks, puzzles to solve, and stories of contradictory wisdom. He was born in that part of the world that was once known as Mesopotamia and the mindset lingered. He used to tell me stories of the villagers where the men of knowhow would fixate their gaze on any horseman of their choice and the man and his horse would tumble down the mountain.

To demonstrate this, he would ask me to pick any cat that was perched on a high wall opposite our garden. We lived in Egypt then, and stray cats used to roam all over the place. They would, however, choose a high wall on which to relax, away from the malicious intervention of humans and dogs alike. The wall opposite our tiny garden was a favourite hangout of theirs.

I always picked one that looked in deep sleep, completely unaware of our presence. The one with the orange spots I might have chosen. Dad would then narrow his gaze and fix his deep, crystalline blue eyes on the selected victim. Within 30 seconds, the cat would jump up in the air with its hair standing on end, its tail bushy; it would hiss and attack an invisible assailant, then make a dash for its life in the opposite direction.

This trick never failed and was my favourite because of its inexplicable and trick-proof nature.

However, at this point in my life, I had once again regressed into default mode. My dire need for a steady and reliable income, reinforced by society's expectations, compelled my mind to consider regular employment. The last time I had to resort to such indignity was when my son was very young.

I remembered the occasion with mixed feelings.

Unlike the rest of my life, my working career had started from humble beginnings as a secretary but I had worked my way up. Through my eager willingness to do and learn anything that came my way, I had placed myself in a position to handle most aspects of private business. The rest I picked up as I went along.

Before we even got married, I had talked my husband-to-be into starting our own business. It happened to be the building industry which neither of us knew anything about. We had built a beautiful home, we had a beautiful child, and within a few years we had a very successful business.

But life being life, and change being the only constant in life, change befell the building industry and we had to look elsewhere. In the meantime, succumbing to the exigencies of life, I had to go back to paid employment to sustain the lavish lifestyle to which we had grown accustomed.

I made an appointment with an employment agency and, to my horror, I discovered I was unemployable because I had been out of the workforce for too long. I will never forget how this scenario unfolded.

"What do you mean too long?" I asked the employment agent. "4 years! What could have changed so drastically in 4 years? Surely my brain cells couldn't have deteriorated that much, I am too young for Alzheimer's."

"Well, I could have grown lazy in those 4 years." "Lazy? How could you go lazy with a baby or young child? You're lucky to get any sleep," I pleaded.

"That's the point I wanted to make," she said. "Mothers with young children are unreliable; they put their children first."

"Yeah, but if you want to run a business as well, you learn to manage your priorities. In fact, you have to be on the ball, professional, and super-efficient," I retorted proudly.

"That's the other point I wanted to mention to you. Employers don't like self-employed people. They're up themselves, they know it all, and can't be told what to do," she added matter-of-factly.

"That's me all right," I concurred. "But I was like that way before I became self-employed, and I still managed to get myself a job."

My powers of persuasion failed me. I went home dejected.

She rang me the next day. "Ah," I said. "I am glad you changed your mind, so you've got a job for me."

"Wait until you hear what it is," she said, sheepishly.

"Don't worry," I replied. "At this point, I'll take anything and work myself up the ladder."

"You might take that back," she said, now defiantly.

"No, I'll take anything," I insisted.

She said cautiously, "Brace yourself. It's a job with a French company ..."

I interrupted. "Fantastic, I speak French fluently … what's the job?

"It's temporary, just for 2 days," she mumbled.

"Don't worry. They won't let me go once they've tried me out. What's the job?" I asked again impatiently.

"A Tea Lady!" she announced, softly.

"That's a cruel joke," I said, soberly.

She explained with a very serious tone. "No, but I am desperate. I have no one else suitable on my books, so I am begging you to do me this service because these are my best clients, and I have to find someone for them for tomorrow."

"And you think I am suitable for a tea lady?" I asked, unbelieving.

She begged, "I am desperate and so are you. Do me this favour, please, please and I promise, I promise I will get you a proper job next week." It was 4:30 p.m., she said. "Think about it. I'll give you a ring at 4:55 before I leave and you can let me know your decision."

As soon as she hung up, I made up my mind. "It's NO." She rang at 4:55 on the dot. I said "OK."

… Was this meant to be a lesson in humility?

~~~~~

EPISODE 16

A battle was now raging between myself and I.

"How could you do this to me? How could you say yes against my resolve?" I chided myself. "I can't do this. I just can't do this. Tomorrow morning I'll ring up and say NO."

The battle between my 2 selves continued all night and neither of us got any sleep. By 6:00 a.m. I was exhausted. I gave up the struggle and "I" faded into "me."

Like a zombie, I had a shower, found myself taking extra time to do my hair and my make-up. I vaguely wondered what she had in mind. I went to my wardrobe wondering and my eyes fixated on the most expensive outfit I owned: a very elegant pant suit. But a pant-suit in name only; it was made out of the most sensuous French silk jersey fabric that moulded around my body and showed every little bump. Luckily for everyone, I didn't have many bumps in those days, just a couple. Then I went to my jewellery box and put on every single piece of gold I owned until I was dripping in gold and finished off with my big gold Spanish earrings. I slipped on my crocodile skin sling back shoes with matching handbag, manicured my nails and toes, and I was ready.

"Ready for what?" I vaguely wondered.

My husband stirred in bed, opened one eye, and asked in bewilderment: "Where are you going at this hour dressed for the academy awards?"

"I am taking the Porsche," was all I could manage as a response. I desperately needed the Porsche to maintain my self-esteem.

I turned up for work early, and the personnel manager greeted me.

"I am here for the temporary position," I started.

"There is no temporary position," she said. "You're in the wrong place."

"The Tea Lady," I feebly uttered.

She took one look at me and said suspiciously, "You don't look like a Tea Lady to me."

"That's half the story," I muttered. "The other half is that I don't even know what a Tea Lady is supposed to do. Can you show me?"

She silently led the way. She stacked up the cups, filled the urn, did everything, while I watched her. Then she explained "You start with the boardroom, there is a very important meeting going on, then you go around the corridors serving the others."

I took a deep breath and pushed the trolley. I opened the double doors to the boardroom and pushed the trolley in. I stood next to it with my hands on my hips. It was the longest boardroom table I had ever seen. All eyes turned on me, jaws dropped.

I was supposed to serve them.

I waited … not knowing what to do.

They waited … not knowing what to expect.

A song played in my head "When she walked in the joint, we could tell she was a big spender, good looking, so divine!"

Whereupon, I took a bow and announced *"Gentlemen, tea is served, you may help yourselves!"*

They all rushed towards me, at once. I had to jump out of the way and take refuge behind the trolley.

Merriment followed, as they all tried to help themselves awkwardly and made an absolute mess, having never had the privilege of helping themselves before. It worked like a charm. Apparently, they had on no occasion enjoyed their tea break so much. They even pushed the trolley out for me.

In the corridors, everyone came out on cue to get their coffee or tea; I suspected they hadn't oiled the wheels for that purpose. I let them help themselves, but my heart sank when this gorgeous Frenchman came out of his office and instantly recognised me. We both worked in administration for a French oil company.

"Mon Dieu, Ani, qu'est-ce-que vous faites ici?" he asked, bewildered.

I explained, briefly.

"Non, non, no, that won't do," he exclaimed outraged. "I am sure we can find you a more suitable position in the company. I'll talk to the others. Meet me for lunch."

He took me to a posh seafood restaurant in the complex where we were working. Soon the other managers and board members joined us. They represented various companies. They teased him about daring to ask me out where they had missed out. He set them right. I got many job offers that afternoon from these gentlemen, but I accepted the one that was created specifically for me by my previous and future colleague.

What started off as the most humiliating experience of my life turned out to be my own version of a Cinderella story.

Instinct and intuition had been the prime instigators of my choices at that juncture of my life, but I had taught myself a great lesson.

The point I had made to myself was that: **your stance in life will determine your behaviour as well as the response you will elicit from others, regardless of outward circumstances.**

~ ~ ~

"I can now use that lesson to make a conscious decision and produce the outcome I desire without leaving it to the Universe to orchestrate such humiliating circumstances, hilarious as they may have been" I told myself and I told Justin.

... It's all in the mindset.

~~~~

EPISODE 17

It went like a charm. The first interview and the job was mine. It was a prestigious company with luxurious offices and a salary to match.

The downfall was the position offered: a Receptionist. It was definitely a notch up from a Tea Lady, so I consoled myself by saying, "They must think me glamorous enough to put me at the front desk of such a glamorous company." Deep down, I felt cheated. "My superior brain power could be put to much better use."

I obviously needed further lessons in humility. As though descending into abject poverty, my husband cheating on me, and being reduced to driving a bomb for a car were not enough.

I thanked the Lord for my son, Justin, and the brand-new roof over my head ... *and, oh, last night's delicious pizza that Justin cooked for us.*

The new job started with a bang. It was Christmas time, and the company put on an opulent show at a 5-star hotel as well as booked overnight accommodation for all staff and their partners so we could drink and not drive under the influence.

Justin and I are normally social drinkers but the abundance of food and alcohol went to our heads, and we celebrated our good fortune by dancing all night and lavishing each other with kisses and laughter.

Good fortune would also have it that Justin worked in the same suburb and we often met for the lunch break and stole whatever sweet moments we could have together while my husband was in town. Justin has an affectionate nature which did not prohibit him from displaying it in public.

This apparently was witnessed by my superior at work and she took particular outrage as it reminded her of how inattentive her husband had become of her good looks and personal charm.

To alleviate the pain caused by her jealousy she took every opportunity to put me down. Of course, I was unaware of what had changed her behaviour towards me. She was the one who had interviewed and hired me, and she was ecstatic to meet someone with whom she could converse in her native French language.

A reign of persecution started and she would go to the extent of going through my desk and rummaging through my waste paper basket after I left the office to go home, with the hope of finding any evidence to discredit me. Her attacks were covert, but she averted any attempt on my side to get to the bottom of the problem with an open conversation.

Though everyone else was absolutely charming to me, which gave extra cause to exacerbate the situation, this one person managed to riddle my life with anxiety. I had to force myself to go to work every morning and could not bring myself to leave because the regular income and the rest of the conditions were so good.

A battle was once again raging within. Tense and on the verge of an explosion, I arrived at work one morning to find my desk drawer had been broken into, the lock on the petty cash box smashed, and the money gone. I turned the computer on but it crashed. I flicked the switchboard on and all the lights started blinking on and off, with bells ringing throughout the 3 floors the company occupied. Employees who had arrived earlier came rushing to my desk wanting to know what was going on.

I spotted the ogre walking towards me with murder on her mind.

"I AM RESIGNING! I AM RESIGNING!" I announced, without prior determination and for everyone to hear.

Just as I finished uttering these words, the bells stopped ringing, the blinking lights stopped, and the computer came on.

Before she could utter a word, I calmly said, "Let me type my resignation first" and proceeded to do so.

I don't remember what happened next, nor do I wish to remember. What mattered was that I was getting out of there, but I had to give 2 weeks' notice. I could cope with that.

Something very strange happened the next day. An announcement came through that our company had just been taken over by a very large American Company. Negotiations had secretly been going on for some time, but it was now official.

The procedure was that everything would continue as normal while the new management decided who would stay and who would go. The ogre was one of the first to be interviewed that morning and was told unceremoniously that her services would no longer be required. She was to clear her desk and be gone by lunchtime.

I watched her leave shell-shocked.

My experiment in conscious control had obviously been a miserable failure, though not without many eye-opening observations.

I decided I was better served to revert back...

... To let go and let the Universe.

⌐⌐⌐⌐

EPISODE 18

"You win," I told the Universe. "But did you have to let me go with such a big bang? What a show you put on! I am chuckling now but it sure wasn't funny at the time. But how you got rid of the ogre, that was a showcase. I didn't see it coming, and there is no way in the world anyone could have orchestrated a more apt exit for her and better revenge for me. All the sweeter because I can blame it on *you* without having to carry any guilt."

"I just hope you have something better in store for me."

"I want you to know I am now putting all my trust in you. I enjoy your sense of humour but sometimes you just push it too far."

I don't know if the above can pass off as prayer but such was the evolution of my relationship with the Universe.

I took a 180 degree turn and embarked on a Reiki course which presented itself to my notice. Healing was what I needed. The Reiki Master, who was a middle-aged woman, grossly overweight, cheerfully announced that she suffered from a multitude of illnesses and elaborated on all the pain and discomfort these were causing her.

She introduced us to a number of her pets, dogs and cats alike, all suffering from one form of terminal illness or other. We didn't need any convincing as the poor animals were visibly in the throes of death.

But I wasn't going to judge.

After further deliberations and some very useful instructions on anatomy and where to place our hands on the body for healing purposes, the initiation ceremony started.

'The Master' recited some mumbo jumbo and spat everywhere (I don't know if this is customary in any other Reiki culture).

"This is …."

"Uh, uh, we're not judging," I stopped myself before I could complete the sentence in my head.

The final exercise of the day was most enlightening. We had to stand in a row, each one of us placing our hands on the shoulders of the person in front of us, to get in touch with what we were feeling. I was the last person but one in the queue.

This was hard. Not only I was not able to get in touch with any feelings, but my arms were getting so heavy, I felt the poor girl in front of me must be crushing under their weight. No matter what I did I could not lift them up. They seemed to be pushing her down against my will. I was distraught at the thought of inflicting this on her but no matter how much I tried, I could not alleviate the weight. "I must be very tired," I excused myself.

Mercifully, the session ended and my agony was allowed to somewhat subside.

The 'Master' then proceeded to ask for our experiences starting with the last person in the row, which was the person behind me. This person light-heartedly explained that her experience was most pleasant, she felt her fingers floating up in the air and she could not keep them down on my shoulders. "So that was not my imagination," I thought to myself.

Without offering any feed-back, The Master moved on to me. I dived into a litany of apologies and I could hardly keep myself from bursting into tears as I explained how very different my experience had been.

"Ah," she exclaimed, rubbing hers hands together. "This is very interesting. You see, the person behind Ani was feeling her energy, which is obviously light and carefree; whereas Ani was feeling the energy of the person in front of her who seems to be weighed down with massive problems. Upon which the poor girl burst into tears, and I felt relief that I was not the source of this weight. "Isn't feeling relieved at the expense of lumbering the problems on to this poor soul perversely selfish?" I remorsefully wondered.

Upon which The Master took the poor soul away, chanted, and showered her with her healing 'spit'. This seemed to do the trick. Our friend felt elated. She then turned to me and with wonderment on her face she said, "Oh, I've never seen an aura before, but I can see yours." "What colour is it?" I asked, not knowing what to say. "It's purple," she said. I had serious doubts.

I didn't wait to the end of the class but rushed away as I had to attend a party given by Ian (my ex-boyfriend) for some charity or the other. The party had started at 1:00 p.m. and it was now 4:00 p.m. and Justin would be wondering what happened to me.

As I pushed my way through some 250 guests, this gorgeous man, towering over everyone else, came towards me with a big smile on his face. "Ah, you're a healer," he announced. "How do you know?" I asked with great amusement, thinking this is a novel pick-up line, I've never heard it before. "It's in your aura," he said. "What colour is it?" I hastened to ask after my previous experience a mere hour ago. "Purple," he said without hesitation extending his hand. "My name is Gary, and I am also in the healing profession. I am a chiropractor."

Any doubt I may have had that Justin may have been a friend of his and had casually mentioned that I had been on a Reiki course vanished when I saw Justin approach us, extend his hand, and introduce himself to Gary.

At the next Mind/Body/Spirit festival, just to make sure, I had my aura photo taken. The haze around my head and shoulders was a distinct purple with a spot of magenta at the top of the right hand corner.

... Obviously, the Universe was conspiring to make a believer out of me.

~~~~

EPISODE 19

The following weekend Justin and I were inspired to go to the Markets. Neither of us had been for a couple of years and we both loved the bohemian atmosphere, where people from all walks of life proudly displayed their art, their craft, and their wares on make-shift stalls huddled against each other.

Walking around nonchalantly, sampling morsels of food from various nationalities that now called Australia home, was a therapeutic way to escape from the drudgery of some aspects of modern life. There was so much to dazzle the eyes and inspire you with flights of imagination to the myriads of possibilities available to humans to indulge themselves, and the opportunities to give reign to their creative impulses, whims, and powers.

At one of the stalls, various figurines of ancient origins were displayed. I fell in love with some of the pieces but could not decide which one to buy. The fact that I didn't have enough money on me was a further deterrent. I asked the person serving if there was a store we could visit on another day to make a purchase.

We were informed there was a young man who was working in a suburb out of town, manufacturing these, but that he had no store to display the products. He gave me his address.

I couldn't put these out of my mind so the following weekend Justin and I drove for over an hour to this remote place to see what was available. The range was extensive, beautiful, and cheaply priced. My curiosity was aroused and the owner, Phil, was keen to show me how these were being manufactured. I was thrilled.

The conversation led to the fact that he did not have a representative to run around to approach garden centres for orders and that he had to divide his time between manufacturing and selling.

Since I liked the products so much, would I be interested in representing his company @ 10% discount so I could add the 10% on as my commission? He asked.

My 2 weeks' notice at work had just concluded on the Friday, and I was free to give it a go on Monday. Was this what the Universe had in store for me? I accepted.

It was a hard slog, locating the various garden centres and carting around so many samples, but I thought it would get easier once I had established rapport with prospective clients, and I could take subsequent orders over the phone.

Within a month, I had done the rounds and had a decent list of clients eager to buy. 10% commission from all the sales amounted to a respectable income.

To my utter dismay and indignation, the following month I found out that Phil had approached my list of clients and was supplying them directly at a higher discount than he was allowing me.

I rang him up to find out what was going on. "These are my clients," he explained. "They are buying my products. You just have to find new clients for yourself."

"But then you will go and supply them directly behind my back again," I supposed.

"That's right," he said. "You just keep on getting new clients; that's your job," he innocently pointed out.

"You can't do that," I said.

"Yes I can," he replied.

Either he was too thick to understand or simply refused to understand because it didn't suit him to do so. I tried to reason with him on the grounds that what he was doing was unfair and bad business practice.

"That's how I operate my business," he declared. "I am smart, and you're not," he added as a plausible explanation.

And that was that.

I felt betrayed by Phil but ever so much more brutally betrayed by the Universe.

... Nevertheless, I felt so very grateful for having Justin.

~~~~~

EPISODE 20

I was helping Marianna organise a tour at a museum in the city, suggested by one of her friends, Jeremy. When we visited the museum, I discovered Jeremy's job there was the production of replicas of ancient artefacts in magnificent finishes of bronze, pewter, verdigris, marble, and rusted iron, and he had the ability to make these look like they were freshly dug out of the ground.

Jeremy's craftsmanship was exquisite.

A light bulb lit up in my head.

"Jeremy, if I give you some ornaments and plaques, would you be able to reproduce them in your finishes," I eagerly enquired.

"Yes, I can do some for you in my spare time," he said. "But I have to make a mould for them first." I gave him a huge hug and pleaded with him to rush the first order.

A few weeks later, armed with a decent sample range, I approached the list of clients I had approached previously. Their expressions of delight at the sight of my samples were more than sufficient to indicate their appreciation of the quality presented to them.

I explained to them that I was no longer representing Phil because I had found out that his garden ornaments, though beautiful, were made out of plaster, which is a substance not suitable for outdoor use. The ornaments would in fact crumble after a while when repeatedly exposed to rain. This happened to be the truth.

We are blessed with copious amounts of water in the rainy season, so I didn't have to insult their intelligence by stating the obvious. However, the next point of sale was dicey to say the least.

I allowed myself to be inspired.

"I want to point out that these products are made out of resin and coated in metallic finishes, which means they can withstand rain and outdoor conditions indefinitely, but they are not anywhere as heavy as products made out of solid metal, cement, or even plaster. They are light and easy to handle and transport costs would obviously be much lower."

They were predictably and invariably impressed, but I had to drop the bombshell, which they were by now subconsciously expecting.

"What's the cost?" They eagerly wanted to know.

I took a deep breath and blurted it out, "It costs more than 10 times as much as the original products."

A deep gasp, followed by a long silence was the usual response. Then came the uniform, dismayed apology. "But we don't carry anything in that price-range, we simply can't!"

Another deep breath and I said: "I know, that's the trouble. A huge number of Australians are now into renovating their homes and following overseas trends. They're going for more up-market looks. Unfortunately, no-one is currently supplying that market in Australia and I have found out, from approaching interior decorators, that they are having to import them from overseas at exorbitant expense. There is a ready-made market and no-one to supply."

As they mulled over this new concept with their eyes turned towards the sky, I offered the clenching solution. "Look, even if you don't sell any, you can use them to decorate and upgrade the look of your shop to attract more clients. If the clients find them too expensive, they will console themselves by buying something from your cheaper range. If they convince themselves they only want the very best, then all you have to do is ring me and place an order."

And before they had any time to work out an objection, I added "For every item in my range that you sell, you will need to sell at least 10 of your cheaper items to make the same amount of profit. Think of all the space 10 items occupy and work out how much rental you are paying for the space occupied by cheap items that erode your profit margin."

They didn't need to work out any figures; they each placed an order.

... Inspired, I was. Now I had to face the music.

~~~~~

EPISODE 21

It was inevitable. The minute Phil found out that I had taken back her/my(?) clients, he was on the phone bellowing his rage.

"You've stolen my clients," he accused menacingly.

"They are now my clients," I asserted firmly. "You just have to find yourself new ones."

"What you're doing is illegal," he warned me.

"That's how I run my business," I explained calmly.

"But I am paying royalties from my sales to a man called Paul for the right to reproduce these ornaments and you're getting them for nothing."

"That's because I am smart and you're not," I volunteered.

"You don't know what Paul is like! When I tell him, he'll hunt you down and bash you up for this," he threatened.

"Thank you for the warning," I offered. "I am now going straight to the police station to register a complaint against you and Paul, and you had better hope to God that no-one ever bashes me up as you will be the first suspects on the list to be interrogated and charged whether you're the ones that bashed me or not."

And I hung up without any further ado.

He rang once more.

"Sue me," was my curt response. "You sell these ornaments explaining the originals are thousands of years old. Don't you think they're way past their copyright date?"

He probably diverted his anger towards Paul who had been extorting him, as I never heard from Phil again.

And that was that. Karma balanced.

I have a confession to make. Despite my bravado, I was shitting in my pants as I didn't know what to expect from one day to the next.

The business thrived but not without its built-in problems. The orders poured in, but Jeremy could not cope with them. Fortunately, my brother, a jack of all trades and master of most, was able to help us with Research & Development.

We started importing exquisite pieces from overseas and hunting antique shops for pieces we could reproduce for our collection. We reduced Jeremy's input to producing moulds. Steve streamlined Jeremy's technique that originally took 6 weeks to produce and set from start to finish to overnight setting where we could produce 20 pieces within 2 hours. We then started to design our own pieces.

We went from supplying garden centres to interior decorators and interior decorating shops. We were being featured in top magazines.

As we got new clients, the orders mounted and the business expanded. It was no longer possible for me to keep Justin and my husband apart.

We operated from our garage, so Justin had to come over every evening after work to cast the figures, even when my husband was home. In the morning, I would apply the finishes I had learned, stack my car to the brim, and set off to sell them.

Justin and I quickly worked out which one of us was suited for what. His meticulous nature was perfect for the precision needed for the casting work. My swift and adaptable nature was put to use in problem solving, selling, and dealing with clients.

I thrived on problem solving, designing, and creating new and better products, but I hated the idea of selling, so I turned it into a game. I would leave home at 10:00 a.m. and head for home at 3:00 p.m. because these were outside peak hours and off-street parking was available.

Before setting off, I would make a list of new retailers I would approach, write down their address, and intend a parking spot right in front of the store if no parking was available on their premises. More often than not, I would go cold calling without a prior appointment.

Invariably, I was told the boss does not see anyone without an appointment. "Really," I would say with a smile. "Just let me show them to you," and before anyone had any chance to object, I would drag in all my wares, have them all over the floor with customers gathering around them, admiring, enquiring, and commenting. I would create such a commotion, the boss would come out to see what was going on and, after some negotiation and explaining why my range was so darned expensive and how that was indeed a distinct advantage, he would end up buying the lot on the spot.

I would then ask for a cheque and would be told their terms were 90-day payment. I would pout and explain I was new to the business, had run out of capital, and needed this cheque to buy the next lot of raw material. Surprisingly, 9 times out of 10 they obliged.

The parking spots never failed me as I was an adept at this by now. I sometimes got lost in suburbs I had never visited before so to alleviate any possible frustration that would take hold of me, I would tempt the Universe "Ah, you got me lost because there is something here that you want me to find." I would then slow down the car, slowing down all traffic behind me, driving the drivers to the brink of rage, and look intently and expectantly. Without fail, I would discover a retail shop that would be a perfect fit for my range of ornaments, which would normally not have been within my spectrum of possibilities.

Some days, when I would feel lazy, I would tell myself: "Let's see how quickly you can make $1,000 so you can go home early. Often, before 1:00 p.m., I had made my $1,000 and I would head home.

Another game I amused myself with, to keep me motivated, was to anticipate what my clients would order next and have these in my car when I dropped in on them impromptu. I would tell Justin, "I want you to cast these next." "Why?" he would ask. "Do you have an order for them?" "No," I would say. "I just know this is what they'll order." Fortunately, Justin was not the argumentative type, and he would comply as long as the 'system' worked. The system did work and money had begun to roll in.

... We dedicated our weekends to celebrating our success.

~~~~~

EPISODE 22

I had been totally insensitive to how my husband felt about our situation. One day, I can't remember what the occasion was, probably my son's birthday, he suggested we take him out to lunch as a family. I slipped a dress on, quickly combed my hair, no make-up, and I was ready to go.

At the bistro, he was uncharacteristically quiet. He ordered some food and when my son went to fetch some drinks, he looked deep into my eyes and with profound sadness in his voice he said: "You look so glamorous when you go out with Justin but look at the way you're dressed with me. You don't care about me, do you?"

I was flabbergasted. Wasn't one of the two reasons he gave for seeking an affair that I cared too much about my appearance?

A few nights later, I picked up the phone to make a call. He was on the extension line talking to his girlfriend interstate. I was about to hang up but decided not to because I was afraid that when he heard the phone clicking, he would accuse me of listening in to his conversations and start a barrage of accusations.

I couldn't help hearing the conversation and got in fact interested because it was all about me. He complained to her about the fact that I am always dressed-up to the hilt when I go out with Justin, but I couldn't give a damn about my looks when he was around. He went on and on about my business and how well it was doing. He figured that Justin was staying with me because of the business. He wondered why such a gorgeous looking man was interested in me when he could have any woman he wanted. He couldn't stand it that after 5 years together (Oh my god, was it really 5 years?) we were still smooching around like teenagers.

He went on and on and on for over half an hour, and all the while she didn't utter one word. Not one word! I wondered if she was still at the other end of the line, except that I could hear her breathing heavily.

I wondered what this conversation would be doing to her. I wondered if he always went on about me. I wondered why she would put up with it.

I was tempted to scream down the phone, "Wake up to yourself, girl. This is precisely the mental environment that promotes cancer. Get out, get out now". But I didn't think it would have been taken in the spirit I meant.

I didn't know then that she had already developed cancer.

The following Saturday, my husband asked me if I could stay the night at Justin's because he had invited some friends for dinner. He also asked our son if he could stay at his girlfriend's place. I was very surprised because he never entertained, but I agreed and even cleaned up the house, set the table for him, and wished him a good time before I took leave.

The next morning, I got a call from my son at Justin's place. "Mom, come quickly," he said. "I just got home and I think we've had a burglar, unless dad has cleared out with the furniture."

Dad had cleared out with most of the furniture and the best of the paintings and crockery and anything of value. My son was distraught, but I soothed him down promising we would replace the lot in no time at all.

Not long after, I got an order from his solicitors to put the house up for sale.

To complete this scenario, I fell down some stairs, broke my arm and damaged my leg so badly I could hardly walk.

Karma was taking its toll.

The prospect of continuing with the business went up in a smoke as we had reached the 5-year point where expansion had become a necessity. Broken physically, mentally, emotionally, and financially, to seek new premises from which to operate and to undertake such a huge financial commitment proved to be beyond my capability at that point.

The house was finally sold, my share of the proceeds would definitely not be sufficient to buy a place for myself and my son. A friend, Viki, offered me a room at her place and my son's girlfriend was happy to have him stay at her place.

At the back of my mind, I had always been concerned about Justin and the gap in our ages. I had spent 5 blissful years with him, but the time had come to let go so he could get married, have children, and make a wonderful father. He deserved that.

I said goodbye to Justin and turned my sight to the future with a vacant mind.

... A vacuum had been created for my destiny to take hold.

~~~~~

PART III
Venturing Beyond

REVELATION 1

Here we go again, back to square one, and I have no idea .... *blank.*

Viki's place was a disaster zone. Her husband, Jed, had for the past several years started renovation projects in every corner of the house. Tools were scattered all over the place but no end in sight was visible for any of the projects.

The first day, I relaxed with a romance novel Viki recommended. I read to take me away from my problems.

The second day, I listened to her problems and how, with no plan in mind, she had lost hope of ever getting anything finished, and she didn't know what to do to motivate her husband to even get started.

The third day, I got matters in hand and devised a complete refurbishing plan for every room, sparing none. I physically dragged Jed to the centre of the house and said to him, "This is where we're starting." The poor man was shell-shocked. He had never met a woman with such resolve. He had no experience at handling such a woman. I took advantage of this weakness and, as I seemed to have no control over my life, I was going to take charge of the one available to me.

By the end of the day, we had achieved so much, Jed's grey cells were ignited and, panting on the floor, exhausted, albeit with great relief and hope at the prospect of getting things moving towards a finishing line, he relinquished all control of the house to me, while Viki took refuge in the kitchen lest thunder exploded inside the house.

My biggest delight in this experience was teaching Viki how to manifest when it came to decorating. I would get her to vaguely imagine what she wanted and put a price tag on it. Viki would come up with a price that even she thought was simply ridiculous. We would then set off willy nilly on a shopping expedition. Regularly, we got lost. As she panicked, I explained to her this was a good sign; it meant what we were looking for could only be found in this locality at that price. The first time, she just raised her eyebrows in total disbelief but said nothing out of respect for all the work I was getting done on her house.

But when, on the first outing, we located a Japanese painting @$20 which would have cost a minimum of $450 elsewhere, her eyebrows expressed a different form of disbelief. Viki didn't need any further convincing. She took to it like a duck to water and together we amplified our positive vibes and went out in search of magic, AND WE GOT IT.

As I put all my efforts into straightening my friends' house and their life, directing Jed, motivating him, and helping him reach decisions, while gradually teaching Viki what to do, how to get involved, and how to stand up to her husband, my own life was falling into place without any effort on my part.

Despite Justin's concerns that our business was no longer a viable proposition to sell, I managed to sell it at a very decent price without giving away our stock. I managed to sell every single piece of stock we had left which amounted to a considerable amount of money, both well beyond our expectations. I managed to get a bank loan despite the fact that I had no source of income. I managed to find a gorgeous little 2-bedroom cottage for myself and my son, for the exact amount I had managed to pull together, with $3,000 to spare.

This gorgeous cottage happened to be situated in one of the less desirable suburbs, on the other side of real estate where the elite live and to which I had become accustomed.

"'Real estate,' I wonder if this is the 'real e(*nergy*)state' of where you really belong" I mused to myself. "Get used to it kid. Obviously, the Universe thinks you need further lessons in humility."

"We'll see to that," I chuckled at my own thoughts and promptly, and with gusto, I got down to the business of turning this place into the Palace of Peace of which I had dreamed. "Build it and your friends will come, and together we will celebrate the best that life can offer *for free.*"

My options were limited but not exhausted.

I was so very grateful for the size of my ego that kept me optimistic, despite the blows circumstances were bent on inflicting on me to keep me down.

The fact that the size of my earthly paradise had been systematically shrinking since my life had turned upside down had not escaped me. What was puzzling, though, was the intensity of pleasure I derived from what was left over, as this seemed to double in direct ratio to the shrinkage of my material wealth. It was as though these earthly possessions carried a weight that you bore on your shoulders and occupied a space in your life, narrowing down the range of other possibilities.

That was a weird **revelation** to say the least. As the weight lifted off, an enormous sense of gratitude descended on me, beckoning me to vistas of realms so far unexplored.

"I wonder what lies beyond" was a quasi-question that entered my mind as I fell into that state just prior to falling asleep and losing complete consciousness.

As if in response to that somewhat vague question, I was granted the head-spinning experience of finding myself lying spread-eagle on a flat disc revolving at enormous speed. Suspended above me, was a huge, metallic, cylindrical object in the shape of an hourglass, spinning furiously in the opposite direction. Through this tunnel within the hourglass, the entire knowledge of the universe was pouring down on me, and I was absorbing it like a sponge.

Suddenly, I found myself propelled in the sitting position in bed screaming out: "By Jove, I've got it, I got it all!"

... *And I was hooked.*

~~~~~

REVELATION 2

Within seconds, that deeply exhilarating feeling of wholeness at the exposure to all the secrets of the Universe had faded into a memory, leaving a gaping emptiness that was impossible to fathom or to endure.

This sense of loss was complete and insurmountable destroying my ego to shattered pieces I couldn't possibly put back together again. I didn't know Humpty Dumpty was an archetypal force.

I felt, though, more of a kinship with Osiris, drifting back to my beginnings in Egypt and the influence on my life by my very first and best Egyptian friend at school, Isis.

Mythology describes Osiris, an Egyptian Pharaoh, as having been killed by his brother Set, who wanted Osiris' throne. Set dismembered Osiris and cut him into 14 pieces which he scattered throughout the land. Isis joined the fragmented pieces of Osiris and brought him back to life and subsequently fell pregnant giving birth to Horus.

Because of his death and resurrection, Osiris became associated with immortality. He is identified as the God of the afterlife, the underworld, and the dead.

But what's that got to do with me?

What an inane question when hollowed me was quickly filling up with infinite questions, seeking finite answers, which not so long ago I held in the palm of my hand so to speak, albeit for an infinitesimal split second of time.

I now knew all the answers were out there. I had tasted them and felt an insatiable hunger for them. All I needed to do was to once again hook up to that source. That's probably how Eve felt when she took a bite of the forbidden apple in the Garden of Eden.

I spent the last cent of the $3,000 left to my name in purchasing a self-development knowledge system which held great promise.

I had a dream in black and white. It was a cold, bleak winter's day. I had seen a poster nailed to a tree promising a reward of 9 Pounds and 6 Shillings for anyone who held the clue to the capture of a certain serial killer. I put on an overcoat and flat shoes, and with my hands deep into my pockets and no luggage whatsoever, I started the walk from Australia to Great Britain to catch the criminal and collect my reward.

"That's a very long walk, let alone having to walk on water to cross the ocean since I can't even swim," I thought to myself in the morning, bemused.

"It's just a dream, not a commitment." I shrugged it off, knowing full well that black and white dreams are the incubating medium of your destiny that crystallise into the light of the day. I also knew that dreams are the portal to other dimensions of reality. That much I had gleaned from my experiences so far.

Freed from most earthly concerns and relationships, now was the perfect time to plunge headlong into this metaphysical reality that was beckoning me like a mythical siren and luring me into uncharted territory.

Bewitched as I was, I settled down to a serious course of study, meditation, and self-analysis, searching within the depths of my being for the knowledge I was craving.

I started by listening, twice a day, to a 30-minute tape I acquired from my hypnosis course to induce progressive relaxation of the body parts to promote alpha states of consciousness. My signal that I had attained a certain level of relaxation was the numbing and tingling sensations I felt in my hands. The further up my arms the tingling sensations travelled, the deeper was the level of relaxation I had reached, and my clue that I had access to a higher level of consciousness.

The value of this tape, above meditation techniques, was the speed with which you could achieve deep levels of relaxation. After a few sessions, the repeated suggestion that in the future, whenever I took 3 deep breaths and counted down from 5 to 1, I would be totally relaxed, was firmly implanted into my subconscious and the process became automatic. I could then produce this effect at call, anytime, anywhere.

In this deep state of relaxation, I noticed that the thoughts that crossed my mind seemed to reveal different interpretations to the ones I had assigned to them previously. It was like the line of my vision instead of being set to one perspective, was set free and would rotate around the thought and show it to me from different angles. Meanings gradually lost their hold over me as I switched from my subjective reality to an objective reality, releasing me from the confines of my limited mind.

I already knew that our thoughts create our reality and that "it is all in the mindset", but how do you un-set a mind that's already set? (My mind kept drifting back to Set who killed Osiris to gain control of the throne.) Obviously, it was a matter of moving from the state of a (Set) rigid mindset, to re-membering the broken pieces of Osiris (an anagram of what truly "is Or is")... *Choices?*

Could the simple act of total relaxation and contemplation of "set" patterns of thought be enough to dislodge them and send them spinning around to reveal the various angles ("or's") and what truly "Is"? This was a new **revelation** to me.

... What else was possible?

~~~~~

REVELATION 3

Having mastered the art of relaxation (alas spasmodically), it was now time to tackle the subject of dreams with serious consideration.

I pondered on the subject without rushing and was surprised to notice that some of my childhood dreams were still as vivid in my mind as the day I dreamed them, whilst I have very little recollection of the actual events that supposedly shaped my life.

The ones that seem to have left an impression on me, yet with no rational explanation, are the repetitive ones. The curious thing about these is that when the ending of the dream changed, the dream ceased to re-occur.

The one that comes to mind started when I was very young, around 5 years of age, and lasted for years. I would be chased by a lion in the desert. I would be running so fast my heart would be about to burst, then I would wake up in terror.

The last time I had the same dream, an ending was added to the original dream. I was running as usual, panic stricken and out of breath and then suddenly in the middle of the desert, a brick wall appeared and stopped me. I could run no further. The lion was right behind me, and I had no choice but to turn around and face it. As it jumped at me, I grabbed it by the jaws and pulled the jaws apart with my bare hands, whereupon the lion turned into a sparrow and I cried and cried because I had killed a sparrow thinking it was a lion.

In hindsight, obviously, I had an issue that was causing this fear and once the issue was resolved my fear was dissolved. However, I was too young at the time to make the connections.

Another dream that persisted for years and years was more complex in nature. My house was divided into two. The front part was bright, modern, and self-contained and that's where I lived. The back part was also self-contained but, in contrast, housed many, many rooms which were dark and uninhabited. All the rooms contained antique furniture, two of each set.

In some of the rooms there were curtains and I knew that behind the curtains there were ghosts. I was naturally petrified and rarely visited the back house, but I knew deep down that this was the most valuable part of the dual-house.

In each dream, the house was different, but the set-up was the same. In the last dream, I no longer lived in that house but now that my son was 10 or 11 (which coincidentally was when my marriage split up), he insisted on visiting it with me. I didn't want to take him there, but I finally succumbed. When he got to the curtain and pulled it to the side exposing skeletons that jerked like puppets, the scene looked so comical that my son burst into hysterical laughter and I joined him. Another fear had been dissolved and the dream ceased to haunt me.

Remembering the dream, it was now clear to me that the curtain or veil of ignorance had already been lifted and that my psyche was clear to explore the unknown, free of fear.

I had now been dabbling with my psyche, exploring its parameters for a while, enchanting myself with its prowess, and was ready to move up another rung of the ladder of consciousness.

Was the world of spirits my next port of call?

I didn't have to look for signs. It intruded into my life in the form of a course in Astral Travel that came to my attention out of nowhere that I can remember.

The course was run by people, some of whom were dressed as monks. I never asked what denomination they belonged to but their teachings were based on gnosis, we were told.

The 8 week course promised to help us develop our capabilities for out-of-body experiences by teaching us how to:

- Develop concentration and conscious awareness with daily exercises.
- Wake up in dreams while already asleep.

- Astral project with several different techniques.
- Protect yourself from negative influences while Astral travelling.

I bought the book on which the course was based to speed up my learning curve. It's entitled *Experiencing the Astral*, an 8 week course by V. M. Beelzebub.

Just as well I had no inkling of who Beelzebub was supposed to represent; otherwise, I would have been disinclined to take up the course. Ignorance in this case proved to be a bliss as the subsequent courses I took up by the same author entitled "Self Knowledge" and "Esoteric Wisdom" happened to be the most spiritually based learning that came my way.

That you are supposed to be able to achieve all this in 8 weeks was a **revelation** to me. Whatever happened to the lifetime of dedication to monk-hood and deprivation, and the surrender to your Master to decide for you whether you are ready or not?

... This course was definitely designed for me.

~~~~~

REVELATION 4

Naturally the sceptic in me didn't believe a word of this but as we were attached at the solar plexus, he came along anyway.

The first session was all about relaxation of the body and the mind to promote separation of consciousness from the body. We all lay down on the floor, the lights were dimmed, and the teacher proceeded to suggest that we relax every muscle in the body starting from the head down.

I was already well-trained in this through my hypnosis course, so I was sold on the idea and went under without resistance. Do not let the word "under" phase you: the deeper you get into yourself, the higher the spiritual realms you access. They are a mirror image.

The next session was about dreams and remembering them.

I remembered the very first dream that had left an indelible impression on me. It wasn't even my dream; it was my mother's.

The story of mum and dad is one of which romance novels are made. They met in an orphanage. Boys and girls were segregated. However, boys and girls who were picked as specially gifted and talented were taken on a camp once a year where they competed against each other in all sorts of sports and mind games. That's where, at the tender age of 7, they fell in love. Every year, mum would beat dad at a competition, and dad would say "I'll get you next time."

At 15, all orphans were relocated as refugees in different parts of the world and both mum and dad ended up in Egypt, separately. They met again by accident (is there such a thing?) and the love story resumed. However, like in all romance stories, they had their ups and downs and, at a down episode, mum met someone else and got engaged to him.

This man lived in a different town and sent a letter to mum asking her to meet him at the train station in Cairo. Dad, who intercepted all her mail, disposed of the letter and met the guy at the train station, punched him unconscious (so the story goes as dad chuckles) put a return ticket in his pocket and sent him back where he belonged. He then went back to reclaim mum's love.

The poor guy was heartbroken, so he married mum's sister, as perhaps the consolation prize. This created a rift between the sisters and my aunt decided to distance herself from her sibling.

Seven years had passed without any communication between them, though they lived within the same suburb. One morning, my mother woke up with a start. "I have to go and see my sister. She needs me. Something is very wrong; someone is dead. I dreamed of this light globe outside my window, and the light drifted up into the sky. My sister is dying, I saw the spirit. My sister needs me," she hurriedly explained and she was out of the door with me in her trail.

When we got to my auntie's house, she seemed to be in perfect health and refused to accept my mother's concerns, making them out to be a ploy for them to reconcile. As they broke into an argument, there was a knock at the door and a policeman announced to my auntie: "I am afraid I have bad news, your husband has been run over by a tram; he died an hour ago."

So it is not surprising that dreams have since held a fascination for me both ominous and intriguing. However, to discover that there was an in-built exact science attached to them was a most enlightening ***revelation*** to me now.

That you could train yourself to wake up in a dream was a novel idea to me. That you could actually change a dream state from the realm of happenstance to an act of will so you could take control of the direction of the dream was an invigorating prospect that sent waves of excitement throughout my entire body.

That, further, creating awareness in the dream state, you could be transported to the higher realms of reality was a dream that could not be. *Or could it?*

This was at once a descent into the subconscious and an ascent into the superconscious. These were states of consciousness I had learned about in my hypnosis course. But surely these belonged in books, not in real life. *Or did they?*

Was the dream state an actual reality? Who orchestrated the dream? Who was the dreamer? How were dreams connected to life and the afterlife? Were they the in-between life? What was their purpose?

… Questions, questions, and more questions.

~~~~

REVELATION 5

Exploring the dreamscape was the subject and object of my occupation and preoccupation till the next class.

Lucid dreams apparently awakened your cognitive faculties and brought awareness not only into the dream state but also heightened these faculties in your conscious states.

Consciousness is a pervasive state. It encompasses the un-conscious, the sub-conscious, the conscious, and the super-conscious. However, there are clear demarcation lines between these states that prohibit transgression from one state to the other.

In the waking state, our awareness is generally limited to the terrestrial conscious spectrum of our mind reality which comprises only 3% of reality. A massive 97% is lost on us as it is veiled from our conscious awareness.

Training yourself to wake up in your dreams opens up the doors to the other dimensions of consciousness, as I was to discover soon.

The first exercise in this training is to question yourself throughout the day as to where you are. This overt and superficially inane question carries the covert suggestion that there are other possibilities available, though unknown, without stirring up the sceptic in you.

Unlike your normal dreams, your lucid dreams are practically indistinguishable from your everyday reality. So your second exercise is to devise a way to distinguish one from the other. The 2 methods suggested are: (1) pulling your finger, and if it extends you know you are having a lucid dream, (2) jumping up, as you will take off in the lucid dream. In the world beyond, the laws of gravity are suspended.

You may feel like an idiot doing this several times a day, but this is a sobering exercise compared to what lies ahead.

The second exercise is to practice awareness as you carry out the most mundane chores of everyday life, like washing, eating, and putting on your shoes. Once again, inane as this may be, this exercise develops the most coveted of all abilities, which is the ability to concentrate, as the focus of your attention is your power point. It also serves to ground your higher senses into the lower ones.

Multi-tasking, alluring and beneficial as it may appear, must never be undertaken as a substitute for focused attention. ADHD is a disorder that's prevalent today because of the many distractions vying for our attention. Order is achieved through the singularity of focus.

I decided to tackle this course as a private investigator to keep the sceptic within disinterested. "We're just playing," I told myself, addressing whichever part of me was listening.

Besides the daytime exercises which included staring at the flame of a candle for 15 minutes a day, coupled with the exercises mentioned above to promote concentration and awareness, I added the nightly exercises of relaxing myself before going to sleep and planting the suggestion that I will remember my dreams.

I started to record these dreams as soon as I woke up and fervently tried to interpret them.

A few days into this habit, I found myself interpreting my dreams to myself while still in the dream state. This became a regular event in my dreams and, unaware of the implications of the phenomena, I was actually developing the ability to awaken within my dreams the critical faculties of thinking and analysing, which are normally dormant in the dream state. This, however, was not covered in the course.

Then, one night, this process of interpretation took on another dimension (excuse the pun). I woke up in the middle a dream, but the dream continued. The dream moved out of inside my head and was projected onto a screen a metre away, in front of me, and suspended in mid-air.

I was fully awake, with my two eyes wide open, watching this dream with huge interest. On this screen, I saw a younger version of me with her back turned to me. She was intently watching and listening to an invisible man. This invisible man (which I must have seen with my third eye – I guess) was explaining things of great importance to her, which I could not hear or understand, but the "me" in the dream could. He drew a line in the sand with a stick and …

… at this point, I could no longer contain myself. "Hey, hello," I interrupted, trying to barge into the dream. "I am here, and this lesson is meant for me, you can't leave me out …"

Whereupon the dream simply switched off.

I was being ostracised. I went back to sleep dispossessed and did not dream.

Just as well I didn't know at the time what the idiom "drawing a line in the sand" meant, as I may have taken the heed and not crossed my boundaries.

In pursuit of knowledge, ignorance can sometimes be bliss was a ***revelation.*** The dichotomy of truth was something that was to be disclosed to me, later on in such pursuits.

*… **Meanwhile, I was going to surrender to my experiences.***

~~~~~

REVELATION 6

I started my Astral travel course on the 1st of July, 2003. On the 4th week, half way through this 8-week course, and after many failures, minor experiences kicked in, starting with dreams of a **different and unusual nature, which left a profound and indelible impression on my psyche.**

Experience A

I dreamed I was at a sit-down dinner function with hundreds of people, elegantly dressed. I found myself gliding above everybody, in the laid back position. I was self-conscious because I was wearing a dress and the position I was in was not exactly demure. Most people were too engrossed in conversation to even notice me, but some did and were quite impressed by this feat.

Experience B

For the first time that I was aware of, I dreamed I was flying. There were a couple of young girls looking at me. I told them to try it, too. I would show them how to, but they declined. I was surprised that anyone could possibly not want to fly.

Experience C

In my dream, I was doing things I never thought I could. I was walking up walls, bouncing on and off them, I was riding things that were flying, I was carrying out so many feats the whole world was in awe. I was famous. I once jumped onto something moving swiftly but couldn't quite make it and crashed; I was happy no-one saw me, but the next one was executed to perfection and the whole world witnessed it.

Experience D

I dreamed I bought a new house. I was excited about decorating it. I discovered there was a river flowing in the basement of my new house. I also discovered several sarcophaguses with Egyptian mummies inside.

Experience E

I dreamed of a pharaoh unrolling in front of me a long scroll depicting all the universal symbols of the cosmos.

Experience F

I dreamed I turned into a cougar. This was the first time I ever dreamed I was an animal. To my surprise, I didn't feel downgraded. Instead, I felt truly powerful as I ran at full speed through the streets of my home town in Australia, and leaped up in the air and landed on top of the highest building in New York. (Such is the supernatural world of dreams!)

I can still feel the power surge in my muscles every time I remember this dream. It felt glorious.

Experience G

I dreamed I was a serpent winding myself up a gigantic tree. This time, I did not feel powerful but instead I felt 'I WAS POWER' itself. In my dream, I analysed the distinction between being powerful and being power itself, and I was filled with wonder.

These were all lucid dreams, but I didn't have a name for them at the time. The shapeshifting exercises were acquainting me with the various modalities of the spirit world. I was being groomed for the next step.

By the way, the film *"Inception"*, though beyond the comprehension level of the average person, depicts precisely the intricacies of Lucid Dreams.

Experience H

After, what I thought was unsuccessfully trying to separate my astral body from my physical body, I gave up. Later, I found my astral body lying across my physical, attached at the solar plexus, forming a cross. I didn't realise what was happening, so, panic-stricken, I tried to bring my astral in line with my body by gradually pushing it through will-power until it clicked back into place.

It was then that I realised I was partially out of my body and all I had to do was to try to get up and walk in the astral, but it was too late, I was firmly back in the physical, agitated. I kicked myself for missing that golden opportunity.

Experience I

Having reached the borderline of sleep and wakefulness, I saw a black animal, a wolf-dog that growled and jumped at me. Fear, coupled with unexpectedness, slammed me back into my body. Only then did I realise I must have been out of my body.

I thought to myself: "Ah, this must be what they mean by negative entities trying to stop you." I was quite surprised that this thought no longer scared me.

It occurred to me that the dream suspended in my bedroom was alerting me to the fact that I was close to the borderline.

The fact that there was indeed a mechanism into place that would deter you from trying to cross this borderline to eternity was a **revelation.** I resolved to overcome my automatic fear and cross this barrier anyway.

Up until then, the majority of my dreams consisted in my attending classes on the other side. Sometimes, I would be running late for a test. Sometimes, I would miss them altogether. Sometimes, I failed a test and the 'Masters' were disappointed in me.

I THEN HAD THE FOLLOWING LUCID DREAM:

I was given a white sheet of paper by the 'Elders' (contract/task?) with a typewritten paragraph of 4-5 lines. I didn't need to read it because I knew the content and had already agreed to it. I knew the content in my dream state but not in my waking state.

One sentence stood out because that sentence was in italics whereas the rest of the text was regular. The sentence ran from midway in the second line to half-way in the 3rd line. It was words to the effect *"I will run the race."*

{I was then side-tracked by another dream within the dream: I had given a party and had invited a lot of people. Cassandra and her daughter were among my guests. I was sure that they would all get along and my purpose in having this party was to introduce them to each other, but I was surprised that they didn't. They found fault with each other, and this was so surprising to me because the faults they were objecting to in each other seemed so trivial.}

Back to the original dream: I was reminded by the 'Elders' that I was chosen to run this race because I can travel at the speed of light whereas the others can't.

I was surprised the 'Elders' didn't look old and wise as I expected them to. They were young (in their 30s in their mannerisms and demeanour but in their 20s in their agility and skin texture.) They were moving fast and were business-like in their attitudes. They were a group of 4 or 5 but one of them was the leader; he was leaning over and handing me papers as they were all suspended in mid-air, above and behind me, not in front of me; yet, I could see them very clearly without turning my head. They were definitely very solid and human in appearance but did not have to talk to communicate. They communicated in writing and thought forms.

They were dressed in robes of a reasonably heavy texture. They wore several layers of clothing. The ones underneath were of a lighter material than the ones on top. The layers got progressively thicker but they were all smooth, not rough. I got the feeling they belonged to another time.

{Once again I was being side-tracked by the party (*procrastinating? distracted?*)}

Back to the dream: I was reminded that I was **chosen** (emphasised) because of my ability to look through the telescope and bring far away things nearer to me and look at them with clarity.

The dream was in colour and had a very earth-like (down-to-earth) quality about it. It did not have the usual fleeting or chaotic quality that dreams have. It was like it was happening in space and time in a sequential, orderly, and conscious manner. I was not simply an observer, and things were not just happening to me. I was managing the dream. Yet this was not a vision, but a quality dream of sorts.

... My astral vision was being established.

~~~~~

REVELATION 7

Without further preliminaries, I was ushered into the Astral World.

Major Experience 1

Before relaxing myself, I told myself "I want to go flying."

I wasn't sure if I was awake or asleep.

I found myself in deep conversation with a childhood friend. Words of wisdom were pouring out of her mouth. I was surprised, as my friend is not well known for her wisdom, though she has oodles of common sense. She sounded more like my sister-in-law who, in contrast, has by-passed common sense in this lifetime and has opted for adulterated wisdom. She is a brilliant concert pianist and most of her time she spends up in the clouds. I doubt that her feet have really touched the ground. I know that her hands have not experienced housework. She often says "I feel like an alien on this planet; I don't belong here." "She doesn't," I concur. My friend, by contrast, is enmeshed in the terrestrial.

This made me suspicious. I took a closer look to ascertain whom I was talking to. It was hard to tell, though the two don't look anything alike. However, their distinctive features were quite clear and they kept alternating.

That's when the teachings came back and the penny dropped: my critical faculties were awake. "Whoopee, this is the sign. I am in the Astral. This is my chance to do some serious flying and sight-seeing." Without further ado, I abandoned my friend/sister-in-law dilemma and got myself mentally in the 'Superman' stance. Only, when I came to lift up my arms, I couldn't find my body.

It was the strangest feeling. I had never experienced a stronger sense of "I" and, yet, there was no substance to me. I looked around for my body but couldn't see it. I wondered what this "I" was.

Just as if in answer to my plea, two disembodied eyeballs with blue irises (which were I/me/mine, yet my physical eyes are brown) popped out of nowhere and turned downwards, emitting two beams of light that zoomed all the way down into my body in bed.

These laser beams, which emanated from this distant nowhere place in the galaxy, shrouded in the deepest midnight blue/black yet light space, where I could see everything with intense clarity, while there was absolutely nothing to see, travelled in an instant all the way down and lodged themselves in a V shape into my solar plexus.

My hands and arms down-under were totally numb and tingling (this usually happens to me when I fall into a state of total relaxation.) I watched from above as the laser beams hit my solar plexus, and I felt my body vibrating like a pneumatic drill, just like my cat Oscar does with excitement when he's caught a possum and my son and I are struggling to free it.

I was above my body and in my body simultaneously. The I/me above saw my Astral body lift out of my body in bed and I couldn't help wondering, "If my Astral Body is still down there, what was up here?"

But I was more concerned with not being able to get out of bed. I was by then a good metre above my corpse, in the horizontal position. "Stop," I yelled. "Enough! I won't be able to get out of bed; I won't reach the floor." (I have no idea who I thought I was issuing my instructions to - I was obviously somehow still stuck in my limited everyday thinking mode simultaneously.) My astral body stopped then and there, probably by sheer coincidence. I wanted to get up quickly and fly before I returned to daily consciousness.

I watched myself struggle into position, and my clumsiness was pathetic. In my excitement, I lost the plot and once again all of 'me's' slammed into my mortal body.

"Shit!"

I realised I stuffed up because of my eagerness, which translated into impatience. Patience is not one of the virtues I had managed to master thus far, so I had put it in the 'too hard' basket, alongside with humility, to work on in my next lifetime. But I decided then and there to make it a priority if I wanted to master the art of flying.

I also knew the goal of Astral Travel is not sightseeing but "What the heck," I had figured. "I am entitled to some fun while I am at it."

The best part of this experience was the lesson, which did not escape me:

The contrast between my friend and sister-in-law did not stop at wisdom and common sense. My girlfriend is a Capricorn, earth sign. My sister-in-law is Cancer, water, the opposite sign. My friend had been living In America for the last 15 years, representing the West and Materialism. My sister-in-law had spent the earlier part of her life in Russia, representing the East and Spirituality. The list of contrasts is endless.

During the whole of the previous week, I had been pondering on the concept of polarities and how one achieves balance or integration. Obviously, not by mixing the opposites. Mixing black and white will give you a murky grey, creating mediocrity. Balance on a seesaw? Hmm, if both sides are perfectly balanced, you come to a stand-still: no movement, creating apathy. I had viewed the matter from all angles but no matter how hard I tried, I couldn't come up with a satisfactory model.

However, what was presented to me in the Astral, were 2 pictures (my friend's and sister-in-law's) superimposed and vibrating, each retaining a dynamic individuality. Yet, when you looked at one picture you could see it receding, while the other surfaced. This happened alternately and at one point formed a conglomerate of the two. You could not tell one from the other; yet, they were still distinctly different. It was amazing. The imagery was brilliant. The message was crystal clear:

TO ACHIEVE BALANCE, YOU NEED TO MASTER
THE WHOLE SPECTRUM OF BOTH POLARITIES,
NOT COMPROMISE THEM.

YOU NEED TO BE AT EASE AT ANY GIVEN
POINT OF EITHER POLARITY.
IN OTHER WORDS,
YOU NEED TO BE ABLE TO MOVE FROM
ONE EXTREME TO THE OTHER,
AND ANY POINT IN BETWEEN,
WITH EASE AND NO RESISTANCE.

FOR INSTANCE,
IF A CERTAIN SITUATION CALLS FOR FLEXIBILITY,
THEN AN ATTITUDE OF FLEXIBILITY SHOULD
COME NATURALLY AND WITH EASE. IF A
DIFFERENT SITUATION CALLS FOR RIGIDITY,
THEN ADOPTING THIS STANCE SHOULD COME
AS NATURALLY AND WITH THE SAME EASE.

OTHERWISE DIS-EASE, THEN DISEASE ENSUES.

OPPOSITES DO NOT NEGATE EACH OTHER;
THEY COMPLEMENT EACH OTHER,
AND BALANCE IS ACHIEVED BY ASSIMILATING
BOTH AND EXPRESSING EITHER ACCORDING
TO ANY GIVEN SITUATION,
NOT BY GIVING UP ONE FOR THE OTHER.

THIS SUPERSEDES THE CONCEPTS OF RIGHT AND WRONG.

EBB & FLOW, EXPANSION/CONTRACTION,
IS THE RHYTHM OF LIFE.

LIFE FLOWS FROM ONE EXTREME TO
THE OTHER AND BACK AGAIN.
THESE OPPOSITES ARE WHAT MAKE
THE FLOW OF LIFE POSSIBLE.

OPPOSITES CREATE LIFE.

THE MOVEMENT OF LIFE IS THE OSCILLATION
BETWEEN OPPOSITES IN THE PHYSICAL DIMENSION.
IN THE SPIRITUAL DIMENSION,
OPPOSITES DISSOLVE INTO ONE.

And what a choice of two people! I had never been consciously aware of the contrast in the two personalities. In fact, their names had never occurred in the same context. The two have never met. And, incidentally, talking of names, my friend's name is Angel, and my sister-in-law's is Lucymona, whom I affectionately call Lucifer (The Bearer of Light).

Despite my unholy attitude at the start of my expedition into this unknown territory, the holy goal of Astral Travel had been achieved: gaining insights. My higher self was obviously and thankfully in charge. My previous moments of serious contemplation had paid off. What a *revelation!*

... I was hungry for more, much more.

~~~~~

REVELATION 8

I didn't have to wait long.

Major Experience 2

I decided to heat up some doughnuts in the oven. I decided to use the waiting time to indulge in some relaxation. I laid in bed and tried to concentrate on my heartbeat, with not much success. My mind kept wandering to the doughnuts in the kitchen. I resolved to give it 10 minutes and if I failed once again, I would console myself with the doughnuts.

I saw this big black bird dive down into my back. "Here we go again, another evil entity." I couldn't recite any invocation to dispel the entity because I had been too lazy and impatient to learn any. I did the next best thing I could think of: I decided not to panic. I said "Damn it, I am not letting you scare me and give up this time after all my efforts." I put the bird out of my mind and directed my attention to the doughnuts.

{I was side-tracked by a dream. A sensuous dream. I realised it was another ploy to veer me away from my goal. I muttered to myself "I wish it was real, but I am not going to get caught up in this dream now and get distracted away from my purpose. This can wait. I have more important things to do now."}

My mind, in its wisdom, fixed itself on the doughnuts and lured me away from my heartbeat, perhaps in an effort to drag me away from my sensuous dream where my heart dwelled. It imagined turning the oven on for 10 minutes, then switching it off and putting the doughnuts in for just another two minutes until they were soft and warm right through and crisp on the outside. I got a waft of the cinnamon up my nostrils and I started salivating. I couldn't wait to fail at my astral exercise so I could have the doughnuts. I took a bite. It was delicious. "Hang on, this doesn't taste like doughnuts; it tastes like an apple. Yuk, I hate apples, but this one is delicious, the most delicious apple I have ever tasted. It tastes just like an apple and yet nothing like an apple." I took a look at the apple in my hand. It was tiny, tangerine in colour, and like no other apple I had ever seen. It looked puny; its appearance would have never enticed me to eat it. "What's going on?" I asked myself. Then the penny dropped: it was the clue I needed, I knew it: "I was either in a lucid dream or indeed had crossed over to the Astral."

"Slow down now, slow down," I told myself. "Remember patience, do not blow it this time". Forget about technique or how it's done just get up and head off, if you find yourself in the Astral, "fantastic" if not, you've got the consolation prize "yum, doughnuts" as Homer Simpson would say, "You simply can't lose!"

I got up and headed for the kitchen. Surprise! I did not go through the corridor; I did not go through the lounge room or dining room. I did not collect 200. "Where am I"? I looked ahead; there was this large room with a few young men engrossed in some sort of endeavour. Uni students, they were. They avoided looking at me. One of them, at the back of the room, looked then turned away. Before I knew it, I was next to him grabbing him by the arm so he wouldn't disappear. "My name is Ani. I am here from Planet Earth. I just want to find out about this place. I only want to ask a few questions," I blurted out.

To my surprise, *he* wasn't surprised. He said his name was Simon (he looked 24 and had blond curly hair) and took me to the kitchen; he put the blind up and showed me outside the window. Everything looked very similar to planet earth, hardly any difference, except that the colours were much more brilliant and you could see the stones the building was made of in a 3-dimensional context, not just the surface. Also, looking down from that level (the 5th?) depth seemed to be much, much deeper … *bottomless.*

Then he introduced me to his parents. I hadn't noticed them before. They were a nice, middle-aged, ordinary couple. She was happily cooking buns. He proudly showed me the masterpiece of his creation. He pressed a button and the bench top she was working on retracted and another bench top slid into place for her to work her dough on.

It was clever; I thought any woman could do with that idea down below. But it was such a clumsy contraption and so noisy, I couldn't stand the racket. I nearly said to him "If in the Astral you can manifest anything by simply thinking about it, why not use a sleeker, quieter model?" Then I thought to myself, maybe his imagination can't stretch that far, and I didn't see the point in offending him. So, seized with the fear that he might be able to read my thoughts, I congratulated him and thought of getting out of there swiftly.

Instantly, I found myself in another section. This section was presented like a Hollywood movie set: rooms next to each other, each depicting a different scene, with no front walls or doors, to allow photographers to shoot the scenes. (*Is that how it's done in Hollywood?*)

The first scene was that of a lonely, skinny, balding, middle-aged man of 57, with sparse, curly grey hair, approximately 6'2", dressed in grey striped pyjamas, utterly depressed and confined to his bedroom, with scarcely any furniture except for a cheap, unmade single bed. Everything in this scene was a pale shade of grey. He was pacing up and down. The intense look of misery in his eyes blocked everything else out of his experience and direct line of vision so that he looked at me and right through me without seeing me. That was a depiction of how he lived the later years of his life and was so stuck in this scenario that he was re-experiencing it as his eternal now.

The second scene was that of a man of 54, very good looking, 6 feet tall. He was wearing a colourful Hawaiian shirt, and his hair was dyed blond. He reminded me of a movie star, but I don't know of any that fit the description. The setting was a walk-in wardrobe, and he was busily rearranging his clothes and deciding what to wear to project a certain image. He was totally self-centred and self-absorbed, and he, too, looked right through me without seeing me. He wouldn't have noticed anything outside of himself, so his world was happily confined to his wardrobe.

The third scene was a sleek, modern apartment. The furniture was high-gloss black. Three women in their late 30s or early 40s were sitting around a table having coffee and sweets and were watching TV. They were wearing jet-black beehive hairdos and looked like relics of the sixties. They were short, overweight, and wearing miniskirts. They looked wealthy and were watching a lifestyle show in Italian. I heard them speaking Greek. They were aware of me and were somewhat annoyed at my intrusion but opted to ignore me. The carpet was black and white like everything else, perhaps reflecting their mental attitudes. I couldn't get over how brilliant the colour black was. As I looked in amazement, I saw a cockroach crawl out from under the carpet. That was it; "I am out of here," I said, "You mean you can't get away from cockroaches even in the Astral?"

As the Astral is of itself insubstantial and what you see is a construct of your imagination and your memories (in this latter case that of the 3 Greek women), the cockroach may have been there for purposes of authenticity as a replica of the conditions on the earth dimension, as ingrained in their memory. It might have also been a ploy to get me out of there as I was getting really absorbed in the Italian Lifestyle Show which was right up my alley, and only a cockroach would have induced me to flee.

The fact that the Astral had an objective reality of its own was a *revelation* to me.

I had seen enough to get an understanding of this dimension and thought of going back. In response to that thought, my Astral Body immediately started disintegrating into sparkly dust but before the disintegration was complete, I had a second thought "Why not hang on a little longer and find out more while I've got the chance?" I instantly regained wholeness and found myself back in the section with the Uni students. They were far more interesting.

I saw a group of young men that weren't there before. They had heard about me and greeted me with eagerness. They too wanted to ask me questions. One of them asked me if I knew Flipper and Big … (?), the names rang a bell but I couldn't place them. I strained to think... *Flipper, Australia...* and as my thought fixated on Australia, I blinked, and in that blink of an eye I was back in Australia, in my body, wide-awake, with no confusion whatsoever as to where I had been and where I was now.

I leaped out of bed and headed for the kitchen. I was craving for the doughnuts. They were 2-bob doughnuts from Woolworths, 3 days old, and normally I wouldn't eat them in a fit.

"What!" The oven wasn't even turned on. I thought the doughnuts would have been burned by now. I couldn't wait for the oven to heat them up, so I decided to settle for the microwave. "20 seconds", I told myself, and pressed the 2-minute button. The doughnuts shrivelled up and turned to rock. I tossed them in the bin. "Just as well. They had already served their greater purpose!"

… I went back to bed full of awe.

⌐⌐⌐⌐

REVELATION 9

Over the next 2 days I thought long and hard about these experiences and what they revealed.

1. The doughnuts had served their rightful purpose. Unbeknownst to me, they became my focal point for concentration, something I was very poor at doing, before. I did not consciously choose to focus on the doughnuts, that gift was gratefully bestowed upon me, with a little help from Above, to enable separation of my Astral from the Physical, as my heartbeat was taking me in the direction of other pursuits.

2. I understood the first section I had visited was of a more spiritually advanced group of people who had consciously decided to spend their time while in the Astral (between incarnations) acquiring knowledge. They had given up their concept of who they were based on physical evidence, and had, thus, regained their youthful energy and appearance as a result, despite their varying ages. The reason they avoided me at first, I understood, was because I looked different to them, the way the spirit of a deceased person (a ghost) would appear odd to us in the earth dimension.

3. The second section was that of people caught up in a scenario of life, duplicating their predominant mental patterns prior to death, who could not let go of that reality. I felt they had been stuck in that scenario for the last 20-30 years (earth time) as an eternal now with varying degrees of happiness/unhappiness according to their degree of awareness.

4. Having had the experience of the Astral with an Astral body, I now understood my first experience was not of the Astral Plane but that of the Mental Plane.

5. The symbolism of the apple did not escape me. Eve ate of the apple and descended into earthly consciousness. I took a bite of the apple to re-enter the unconscious.

6. I absolutely love the ingenuity and sense of humor behind my experiences, whatever their source. I get the distinct feeling that I am being taught and being helped by unseen presences, whose nature I am not sure of. I have not yet encountered anything outside of me, except for humans in transit in the afterlife. However, the insights/knowledge/understanding feel as though they are coming to me from an outside source. Inside and outside are almost interchangeable.

7. The most bewildering aspect of Astral Travel would have to be The Crystal Clarity of that sense of "I." The quality of the "I" in that other dimension of reality is crystalline. It feels as though if you flick it with your fingers it will reverberate throughout eternity and impose the wave/sound/pattern of its essence on the whole universe as it expands. I don't know how else to explain it.

8. Astral Travel is quite, quite distinct from dreaming and these are my findings:

   • When in the dream state you have no control over what is happening to you and things seem to happen to you. You seem to have lost your analytical powers, your faculty of reasoning, your will power or freedom of choice. Your emotions dominate your total experience.

   • In Astral Travel, you retain your consciousness and thus can be in complete control of what is happening depending on how well you direct your mind. Your experiences will be in direct response to the conscious direction of your mind or your predominant thought patterns. Everything feels just as real as in the earth dimension and everything makes complete sense, in complete contrast to the eerie quality of dreams where everything happens without any rhyme or reason.

- The memories of the Astral stay with you intact, unlike memories in the earth dimension which fade in time, and memories of dreams which fade in no time.

- When you enter the realm of dreams, you shut down your intellectual faculties, the frontal cortex becomes dormant, and you enter the subconscious, which is ruled by the mammalian brain of emotions.

- When you enter the realm of the Astral, you have to go through the realm of dreams, and sometimes the two get confused until you learn to distinguish one from the other. The portals to the Astral are through the dream realms and the lower realms of the Astral are very similar to dreamlike conditions, but as you gain more clarity of thinking you move to the higher realms where everything gets brighter and clearer until you reach the mental realms where projections of the mind become superfluous and you can think with complete clarity without the aid of mental images. This is where you experience the sense of "I" with that exquisite quality of clarity, totally devoid of doubt or confusion, where "I am" is all you need to experience without the necessity for adjectives or attributes.

- Beyond the Mental realm I have an awareness of the realm of the unconscious where the archetypal prototypes dwell. I am still waiting for divine intervention to find my way there.

These insights were a major ***revelation.***

*... **Understanding was culminating into knowing.***

~~~~~

REVELATION 10

That wasn't all.

Major Experience 3

I took 3 deep breaths and counted down from 3 to 1. In 'no time,' I was transported to a desolate dimension within the land of eternity. Everything here was in dark shades of grey. I witnessed a herd of people being swept away by a visible current of wind in undulating shades of grey. These were men, women, and children dressed in rags, covered in dust, shielding their eyes with their arms. They were desperately fighting against the direction the wind was pushing them.

I was overwhelmed by their collective, intense feelings of despair. I could feel their agony as though it was mine.

"Who are these people?" I asked my constant invisible companion on these astral journeys to which I was now accustomed.

"These are victims of bombings," came the chilling answer without words.

No further explanation was necessary. It was suddenly clear that these were the people of 'no choice.' They were being swept away by their own despair, morphing into the winds of their fate. They were people who believed they had no options in life except those handed to them by others they accepted as their rulers and saviours. Their fate was sealed by the inactivity of their minds and lack of personal will power.

I thought of the millions of anxious, innocent, young people sent to war in the name of glory, with the promise of freedom, when in fact they were being used as fodder to feed the lust of the warlords of greed and insanity.

"Innocence and ignorance should not be synonymous," I pleaded in vain.

Brief as this scenario was, it was all-encompassing in its message. No wonder the ancient civilisations were so obsessed with death and the afterlife. It is not until you have a full grasp of these, can you make sense of life on earth and the choices available to us. We have lost trail of this knowledge at our own peril. War is such a permanent fixture of the human condition that we have become desensitised to it and accept it as normal.

Religion has taken over as a control mechanism by instilling fear into our hearts, with a 'Reward and Punishment' system of belief that numbs our minds and renders us victims to their promulgators. Our governments do not govern; they seal our fate with their hidden agendas.

The Passage to Hell is littered with Holy Belief Systems.

We are stripped of all power to forge our own destiny. No wonder occult knowledge and gnostic systems of belief were banned and death was imposed upon their followers.

Occult simply means hidden and knowledge is power. Power resides above the realms of duality and is neutral in essence. It can be used for good or it can be abused as evil.

Our rulers use this knowledge to their advantage while cleverly manipulating us into submission by vilifying the sources of this knowledge and getting us to wage war on each other with the sheer intent to suppress the possibility of such knowledge to take hold.

Despite being surrounded by billions of people, life on planet earth is a solo experience for each and every one of us. And each and every one of us has to undertake this journey of self-discovery for the salvation of the self and the salvation of the whole of humanity. The two are intrinsically interconnected.

I felt a compelling urge to share this knowledge. I didn't know where to start or what to say. Who would believe me? I sat at the computer thinking I would write my story or perhaps integrate it into the material for the 'Practical Life Skills' workshop I was running at the time. *But where do I begin?*

My mind went blank, and my fingers started moving. What came out bewildered me beyond words. As I read back what I had just been typing, I kept wondering where this information was coming from. "I didn't know I knew this," I kept repeating to myself every time I read back the latest chapter I had just written. Yet, paradoxically, inwardly I knew that I already knew it all. It had been poured down on me through the hourglass of my astral vision.

As soon as I moved away from the computer, the knowledge would sink into oblivion and I could not verbally communicate it to others. The minute I sat at the computer with the intention to hook up to this knowledge, the information would be automatically transmitted to my fingertips, bypassing my intellectual faculties.

I called this the 7th Sense, hence the title of the first book I wrote which was virtually downloaded automatically:

The Seventh Sense
Your GPS to the Cosmos

This was like reverse engineering the astral projection process. I no longer needed the process of the Out of Body Experience (OBE) to access this knowledge. I was already hooked: hook, line, and sinker through my nocturnal expeditions to the other side and the esoteric schools I had attended in my dreamtime.

Writing had become the medium of communion with this knowledge and the means to communicate it to others.

Fate or Destiny?

As I've come to understand it:

Fate is a position of limited choices, feeling stuck within the confines of a linear 3-dimensional reality, where the circumstances of your life seem virtually out of your control.

Destiny implies a destination, a conscious direction in life and a vertical expansion of consciousness, where seemingly higher powers collaborate to help you reach your chosen purpose in life.

It was finally glaringly obvious to me that, in response to my avid quest for esoteric knowledge, the Universe had been conspiring all along and managing the circumstances of my life by throwing me into situations uninspired, uninitiated, and often unwelcome by me, with the ultimate purpose of making a writer out of me and aligning me with ITS will to share this knowledge.

... WHAT A REVELATION!

Conclusion

The manuscript for "*The Seventh Sense – Your GPS to the Cosmos*", which was completed early in 2004, sat on my desk for 9 years, collecting dust, until I had the courage to self-publish it on Amazon Kindle as an eBook.

I did not think the world was ready to accept it yet. The reality is I was the one who was not ready for exposure. A lot of its content has since become mainstream, and finally, 10 years later, I am ready to come out of the closet.

I no longer care how people judge me and my experiences. My mission is to put it out there and what you make of it is entirely up to you.

"*Fate or Destiny?*" is the sum total of the experiences (hilarious in retrospect) that led me to some very serious discoveries. These discoveries are related in great detail and in much more depth in my first book, "*The Seventh Sense,*" where my personal experiences are totally absent and practically irrelevant.

These insights are further explored in my subsequent book "*Meet Jesus The Alchemist*" and my 3 books in the Q&A Series.

Astral projection can be a lot of fun; and fun is part of our entitlement to our exposure to 3rd dimensional reality, and most OBE experiences are confined to those dimensions where our main interests lie.

Access to the higher dimensions is of crucial importance if we have any chance of understanding life and how to live it. How we conduct ourselves here, how we think, and how we feel determine exactly where we end up on the other side.

Conversely, what level we reach on the other side also determines the conditions we are born into on re-entry to the Earth Dimension.

Life only makes sense once we understand death. Death is a transition from one state of consciousness to another. You don't have to die to experience what's on the other side. The sincere seeker will find the way.

My journey has not come to an end yet; only this phase has. I am now being exposed to further realities that, I confess, seem well beyond my capacity to fathom or assimilate.

However, if the Universe decides to once again collaborate with me, the secrets to the Origins of Humanity will be revealed, and I will let my fingers do the sharing.

Meanwhile, if you are interested in finding out more about the insights gained from my astral experiences, which are well beyond the scope of this book, you will find them by googling Nano Daemon or on Amazon.com by searching for books by Nano Daemon.

One Last Thing

If you derive any benefit from this knowledge, I would truly appreciate it if you left a review on amazon.